MENTOR *us*

A GUIDE TO EQUIP COUPLES FOR MARRIAGE THROUGH THE ART OF MENTORSHIP

Tom Goodlet & Carol Burmood

with Matt Gardner & Heather Gilstrap

Published by Two Penny Publishing
850 E Lime Street #266, Tarpon Springs, Florida 34688

ISBN: 978-1-950995-19-6
eBook also available

FIRST EDITION

For more information about this author or to book event appearance or media interview, please contact the author representative at: info@twopennypublishing.com

This book is dedicated to all the Marriage Mentors at Harborside Christian Church who rose to the challenge of equipping couples for marriage. Without you there would be no book, no mentorship program, no ongoing smiles from Mentee couples who now have a clear vision for their marriage. Thank you for the work you have done. Now this material can help and empower many more couples.

TABLE OF CONTENTS

Introduction

WHY THIS BOOK?

Welcome to *Mentor Us*. We built this material in conjunction with building a wedding chapel at our church, with the purpose of equipping engaged and newly married couples with the skills and mindset for a successful marriage. We originally created this material for couples within our church who are in a healthy marriage to work with newlywed couples through a mentor relationship. Maybe you picked up this book and you don't know about Harborside but you care about your marriage. Here are two popular questions we can address right away.

CAN WE USE MENTOR US IF WE ARE ALREADY MARRIED?

Absolutely yes! While we initially designed *Mentor Us* to equip couples who are about to be married, we have also used it to help already married couples strengthen their marriage. It is a great marriage enrichment tool for any marriage. The principles are timeless and the activities are good marriage strengthening exercises. Just don't get hung up on all the wedding and pre-marital language. You can navigate around those engaged couple's terms and get to the heart of the principles, concepts, and exercises. So feel free to adapt the book as needed in order to take your marriage to a whole new level.

IF WE NEED MENTORING, THEN WHO SHOULD MENTOR US? OR, IF WE WANT TO MENTOR ANOTHER COUPLE, THEN WHO SHOULD WE LOOK TO MENTOR?

At our church, we have staff who help pair up Mentor couples with Mentee couples. But what if you do not have that luxury? What if you have no clue as to who should mentor you? What if you want to mentor another couple but you are not sure which couple would be the best candidate?

The good news is you are in the best position to select and decide who should be your Mentor or Mentee couple. You can look at the couples you know, and with the help of some clarifying questions, you can make a CLEAR choice as to the couple you want to invite along on this journey. Here are some questions that will better your chances of success when making your choice.

A Mentor couple is a good fit when they are people who:

easily **C**onnect — With which couple do we have chemistry? With which couple do we naturally bond and enjoy being around?

are **L**earners — Which couple always seems to be learning something new and sharing that information with others? Which couple has the type of marriage that we would like to have some day? From which couple could we learn the most?

are **E**xciting — Which couple brings an energy, motivation, and/or drive with them? Which couple would we be excited to have as our Mentors?

are **A**uthentic — Which couple is real about their marriage and honest with us?

are **R**eliable — Which couple will show up, invest, and participate with us?

A Mentee couple is a good fit when they are people who:

easily **Connect**   With which couple do we have chemistry? With which couple do we naturally bond and enjoy being around?

are **Learners**   Which couple could really learn from us? Which couple seems to want to learn and apply any new knowledge they receive?

are **Exciting**   Which couple brings an energy, motivation, and/or drive with them? Which couple would we be excited to have as our Mentees?

are **Authentic**   Which couple is real about their marriage and honest with us?

are **Reliable**   Which couple will show up, invest, and participate with us?

We encourage you to seek out a couple who models a Christ-centered life. Your Mentor couple should possess fruitful life experience you desire to see in your own life– that can be in their faith, their marriage, or maybe how they raised their children. Your Mentor couple should have the kind of experience and reputation that would make you want to become more like them.

Once you identify a CLEAR choice for your Mentor or Mentee couple, it will take a little courage to ask them if they would like to join you on this journey through *Mentor Us*. You might feel nervous or fear rejection, but that is all a part of the experience, and it adds to the excitement when they say, "Yes!"

WHY THE CHAPEL?

BY KURT PARKER, SENIOR PASTOR AT HARBORSIDE CHRISTIAN CHURCH

The vision for the Harborside Chapel and the *Mentor Us* mentoring program was inspired by God Himself, but it took a number of years to formulate. Let me explain.

In my nearly forty years of ministry, I have performed many weddings for couples—probably hundreds—but I realized I wasn't equipping them for marriage. That realization came when Danita and I had been married about 15 or 16 of our now 37 years, and it just clicked with us, "We're not very good at this whole marriage thing... and we're 'professional Christians!' What is wrong, and what are we missing?" We began to ask God to reveal it.

He showed us a couple of things. First, it isn't about love. Everyone who is getting married is in love, but love doesn't guarantee a happy marriage. Second, it takes skills. People who stay married really have different skills from people who don't stay married. It began to dawn on me that even those who aren't Christians stay together, so it had to be more than faith. Depending upon your home life and how you were raised, those skills would be the game-changers. It had to be about skills, skills, skills. We began to ask Christ to reveal to us what skills are necessary for marriages to succeed.

We felt confident that God wanted Harborside, by teaching people the skills for marriage, to change the trajectory of marriages in our community and throughout the state of Florida. To do that, we would not "just do weddings"... but equip people for marriage.

So, the focus became, how can we help people have the skills for marriage—skills needed to make their marriages work—and set them up for success. Sometime in 2012-2013, God began to set the second phase of the vision in process—for us to build a wedding chapel on our property, one that was drop-dead gorgeous and beautiful in order to attract as many brides as possible. We want to share with couples that God has a plan for their lives, especially their marriages.

I immediately took the idea to our elders. Now the elders were used to me coming to them with big ideas and crazy thoughts, but they all pretty much looked at me as if to say, "All right, tell us why we would do this." To their credit, they didn't ask me how, but why. I loved their honesty, their love. They were spot on with the questions. Why would we spend a lot of money to do this for people who don't even attend our church? That was a great question. And then very quickly, they caught the idea of reaching people with skills and the gospel, and teaching people that marriage actually comes from God. The "how" became a little bit more challenging, and that took a couple of years for us to work through. But again, one by one, the mental lights went on; and we were totally united before we ever started the project.

They had caught the vision.

This was something no church that we're aware of had ever done—built a wedding chapel primarily for the unchurched, as an outreach. We would actually raise capital and attempt to get our entire congregation united in a line over an outreach mission. As with any project like this, there are always early adopters, and some early adopters saw the vision. But also in any project that has not been done before, your percentage of early adopters is relatively small. The biggest challenge we had was trying to help the congregation to see we were not doing this for us. We had to say that over and over and over again. We were not building a wedding chapel for us. We would be building it to attract every unchurched bride we possibly could in our community. After about a year or so of teaching that vision, people began to get it.

Another huge obstacle we had to overcome, given our particular situation, was, "Why are we building a wedding chapel when we need to build a new worship center? We do not have enough space now." Again, people really had to understand that we weren't building a chapel for us. We were building it for others who were lost.

As our plans began to formulate, it became apparent that we didn't want to do marriage counseling; marriage counseling implies there's a problem—the 'wheels have come off.' Our goal was to get in front of the problem. How can we reduce all these social issues? How can we reduce all these community problems? How can we…?

So, if we weren't doing marriage counseling, what vehicle would we use to equip people for marriage to help them succeed? We decided early on that everyone who committed to having their marriage ceremony in the Harborside Chapel would attend our mentoring program.

We quickly realized as we were considering materials we would use that most books, materials, and articles on marriage addressed the "hows" but not the "why." Yes, it's important to tell couples the "hows" of marriage—how to fight fairly, how to have a budget, how to get along, how to deal with in-laws; but it's even more important to tell them the "why" of marriage—because it was God's idea! That's where this book you are holding, *Mentor Us*, comes in. And that is why our introductory session to the material, which is usually led by the pastor who will be performing the marriage, is entitled "Why Marriage?"

Once couples understand the "why" of marriage, they are going to need help to put it into practice. That is where our Marriage Mentors come in!

Marriage Mentors are the key to the whole mentorship process. Every couple getting married through Harborside or in the Harborside Chapel is paired with a Mentor couple who leads them through a number of sessions. Marriage Mentors help to provide some stability, structure, and examples of what marriage can be.

Were there some surprises along the way? Yes, I think the number of weddings we have contracted has been a surprise. Since God was the one who gave this vision to me, I knew He was going to be wildly successful. And, I had the benefit of hearing His voice to know what was coming, and I knew the weddings were coming. I kept telling our chapel team that we were going to have a lot more weddings than we were prepared for. In fact, I bet our Chapel Executive Director a glass of unsweet iced tea from Starbucks that we would have a certain number of weddings the first year... and I won because we far exceeded that number. I keep on betting with him, and the weddings continue to come.

The Harborside Wedding Chapel began as a carrot to brides, but it's truly become an anchor of our church. We are trying to help these couples with one of the most important institutions God has given to us—the sacrament of marriage. We are blessed with skilled and godly Marriage Mentors who are pouring into all these couples.

Our goal through the entire process is to get people to fall in love with Jesus Christ. If we get couples to do that, their lives will change—he'll be a better husband and dad, she'll be a better wife and mom, they'll be better co-workers and better business leaders.

Would I do it all over again? Absolutely!

WHY MARRIAGE?

BY TOM GOODLET, ASSOCIATE PASTOR AT HARBORSIDE CHRISTIAN CHURCH

Why did God create this thing we call marriage? You heard me right. God created marriage. It was not some land swapping concept that developed out of the Middle Ages. The idea of marriage and weddings showed up in written word over 3,000 years ago in the Old Testament. In the first few chapters of Genesis, the first book of the Bible, we see a man and a woman become husband and wife under the supervision and authority of God. Humans did not invent marriage. God did. God created marriage and gave it to us. And, as much as we sometimes make fun of it, groan about it and pick out its flaws, over 90% of us will do it. That's right. The vast majority of us will be or have been married during our lifetime. And we will dream about it, write songs, sonnets, and movies about it. We will cheer it on for others and spend a lot of money on it ourselves. Why? Why did God create marriage—a union that we somehow cannot seem to help but be a part of it?

As we explore this question a little further, we find at least five major reasons why God created marriage.

1 God created marriage so a man and woman would experience companionship.

In the very first chapter of the very first book of the Bible, is the story of a Creator God creating creation. After everything God creates, He exclaims, "It is good!" God creates some plants, and He says, "It is good." God creates some birds and fish, and He says, "It is good!" God creates some more animals and us, and He says, "It is good!" And then Genesis chapter two rolls along and for the first time God says something is not good;

"It is not good for the man to be alone..."   —Genesis 2:18

Notice God does not say, "It is not good for the woman to be alone." Maybe she could use a break. Who knows? Just some fun food for thought.

Either way, God is onto something. Did you know married men statistically live longer than single men? It is not good for men to be alone unless you want to die young.

God's solution to man's loneliness is not a dog, not a TV with the NFL network, and it is not even a best bro. God's solution to man's loneliness is to create and present him a woman;

> "So the Lord God caused the man to fall into a deep sleep; and while he was sleeping, he took one of the man's ribs and then closed up the place with flesh. Then the Lord God made a woman from the rib he had taken out of the man, and he brought her to the man." —Genesis 2:21-22

The dumb pastor's joke that usually proceeds this passage goes; When God presented the newly created, naked lady to Adam, Adam was like, "Whoa-man!" And that is how she got her name.

So, God presents the woman as a wonderful, much-needed companion to the man. When I do weddings, I often like to include the following thought:

Notice God created woman from man's side. Not from his head so he could rule over her, not from his feet to be trampled by him. God chose man's side where woman would be equal with him, under his arm where man could protect her, and close to his heart where he could hold her dear.

So why companionship? Why do we need someone else? Let's first start with something we know does not work out well for us—autonomy. I spent some time on this topic in another book I authored called *Blind Potential*. Here is an excerpt on autonomy:

"Autonomy is a lie. Autonomy is the idea that you do not need anyone else; you can fully stand on your own. It is easy and somewhat natural to pursue autonomy. People want to self-govern, individuals want independence, and each person wants to be accountable to no one. While these ideas are not in themselves horrible, they are not completely attainable nor accurate in the happiness they advertise.

It is interesting to me that men, including myself, desperately chase autonomy.

A man often wants to be his own boss, his own authority, his own independent man free from the support of others. The problem regarding autonomy is that it is a blatant lie. Even if you are the CEO, you are accountable to a board or shareholders. If you own your own business, you are accountable to your customers. Recently, a man who started his own business told me, "I decided to become my own boss, and instead, I took on hundreds of bosses." He knew if he stopped pleasing his customers, he would have no business left. Autonomy is a lie because people will always need other people to succeed, and there is nothing wrong with this truth; everyone on this planet has something—some condition or struggle—making them dependent on other people. Every someone needs to rely on someone else."

We were created for community. How do I know this? Because in Genesis it tells us we were created in the image of God;

> "Then God said, 'Let us make mankind in our image, in our likeness...'"   —Genesis 1:26

Why does God use the words "us" and "our" when discussing among Himself? Because even God has community. The Scriptures describe God as Father, Son, and Holy Spirit. God has His own community. If we are created in His image, then we need one too. You are not meant to go through this life alone. You are meant to be together with your spouse, growing old together and growing deeper in your understanding of each other. There is just something wonderful about waking up in the morning knowing you are not alone as you face the world's circumstances ahead. Marriage is one of God's great ways to provide us with companionship.

Notice the word is "complement" and not "compliment." "Compliment" means commenting to each other with sayings like, "Baby, you look fine in that dress." or "Honey, your strong arms make me feel weak in the knees." Don't get me wrong, compliments are good. We should all give each other compliments. However, God does something even better through marriage by allowing us to complement each other.

> Genesis 2:18 says, "The Lord God said, 'It is not good for the man to be alone. I will make a helper suitable for him.'"

Let's talk about the word "helper," which shows up in this verse. This word is taken from a Hebrew word, written in a Hebrew text, and then translated into English. The problem with the English translation is some people can see the word "helper" and think of someone who is subservient or lesser in some way. That is not at all what the term means. In fact, God uses this same Hebrew term to describe Himself in later scripture, in the Psalms. We know God is in no way weak, and neither is the true definition of this word. It is a term representing someone who is strong where the other person is weak. God creates woman to be strong where man is weak and vice versa. Marriage, as we see in the beginning, is God's way of complementing us. The man and the woman bring areas of strength into the relationship to compensate for some of the existing weaknesses. The man and woman are both unique individuals who have the opportunity through marriage to bless one another and complement one another with his and her talents, gifts, abilities, and perspectives. It was probably explained best in the movie Rocky, when Rocky Balboa tells his future brother-in-law Paulie why he adores his soon to be wife Adrian so much when he says, "She's got gaps. I got gaps. Together we fill gaps."

Now notice we chose the word "complement" and not the word "complete." The idea that a couple completes one another shows up in books, magazines, social media, TV shows, and movies. There is that classic scene in the movie Jerry McGuire where Tom Cruise tells Renee Zellweger, "You complete me." And then all is fixed in their story, and we assume they live happily ever after with each other. The problem is we don't and won't complete each other; it is an unfair and impossible expectation to put on your spouse. And yet we still do it. We get in our heads that we are looking for a soulmate who will make our lives feel complete. They will somehow bring us ultimate satisfaction. All we have to do is find them and marry them, and the rest will be perfect. And so, we attempt it. We fall in love. We marry. And one day, we wake up and acknowledge we don't feel satisfied with our life—there is something missing. We don't completely like our life and conclude it must be our spouse's fault. They are not satisfying us. They are not making us feel complete. "Oh no!" we think to ourselves, "I must have picked the wrong person. I thought they were my soulmate, but obviously, I was wrong, or else I would not feel this way." So, we tell them we want a divorce and go for round two.

Only God can complete you. That's right—God reserves the opportunity to bring you a sense of completeness and satisfaction for Himself. He is your soulmate. He designed you and me, all with a need for a relationship with Him. Only God can fill that God-shaped piece that might be missing in your life. Only He can live up to the expectation of actually completing you.

One of the ways God uses the vehicle of marriage to complement us is by creating within us an attraction to someone who is often very different from us. Did you know, statistically, there is only one human relationship where we tend to attract and bond to our opposites? Often the friends, coworkers, neighbors, and siblings we hang out with the most are very similar to us in personality and interests. There is only one human relationship where this is commonly not the case. That's right—the mate relationship! When it comes to a mate, opposites attract. Now we don't always notice these opposites upfront or as we fall in love. We just dismiss them away. We say, "She's just quirky," or "He just has an interesting way of looking at life." "She's a rare find." Or "He is so mysterious." Later in marriage, these sayings can change to "She's so annoying." Or "He's an idiot." Over time the fog of love can wear thin, and the opposites that were there at the beginning of the relationship are now more obvious. What was once attractive and interesting, is now somewhat repulsive and getting old fast. What complicates the situation further is when we chat about our frustrations with our close friends who are wired similar to us. They don't understand our spouses any more than we do, because they are wired more like us. So, when we share what we observe about our spouses, our friends may pile more fuel on the fire by saying, "She sounds crazy." Or "He seems to be acting like a jerk." Our close friends won't often get it any more than we will.

You will either learn to complement each other or complain about each other, which is the kiss of death for your relationships. In all reality, you don't want to be with someone who is just like you. Then you will have bigger gaps and issues. If you can embrace the differences, you win. That is why it is important for the couple to learn to work through their differences together.

And work it is. Marriage is work. Great and lasting marriages take hard and consistent work. Have you ever been to an event where someone from a stage surveys the crowd by asking how long each couple has been married? We clap for those married over ten years. We hoot and holler for those couples who have been married for over twenty-five years. We give a standing ovation to any couple married over fifty years because there was no way that was easy. These are two very different people who, instead of using their differences to push them apart, they used them to complement and compensate for each other. They brought their unique skills, gifts, perspectives, and abilities to cover for each other, bless one another, and carry their marriage through the good days and the not so good days. They must have worked hard to be together for that long.

How hard are you willing to work? Please forgive me if I negatively mention a car you own, but here is the question. Would you rather own a Ford Fiesta or a Ferrari? The Ford Fiesta is one of the cheaper made cars on the market. It is cheaper in purchasing price and its parts that make it up. When something breaks on the Fiesta, and it will, it will be cheap to buy the necessary replacement cost. It was listed as one of the most unreliable cars of 2018. You do not have to spend a ton of money upfront on a Ford Fiesta. And at the end of the day, that is what you will have, a cheap, low-value Fiesta. (Again, sorry to all the Fiesta owners out there.)

What if you decided to own a Ferrari? It will definitely be more expensive to purchase. If something ever breaks on it, the replacement piece will be expensive. However, at the end of the day, you will own a Ferrari. By the way, Ferraris are some of the only cars known to accrue in value over time. The Ferrari will be more expensive and, at the same time, more valuable. What kind of marriage would you like? The Ford Fiesta kind or a Ferrari type? You decide this now, early on in your marriage. It will determine how much time, money, and energy you will invest in your marriage. If you want the Ferrari type marriage, then it will require more of all three. This means budgeting for date nights, weekend getaways, and couple's vacation. This may also include other investments like a swing on the front porch with seats for two, furniture you can cuddle on, and an unlimited lingerie budget. All of these are not expenditures as much as they are investments. Why not go for the Ferrari? Maybe you will get a standing ovation in fifty years.

3 God created marriage so a male and female would be deeply connected.

Did you know, statistically, the number one fear of most women is abandonment, and the number one fear of most men is failure. That's right; even in our fears we are different. So, God gives us the opportunity, through marriage, to not just compensate for each other's fears but to connect in ways that put our fear to rest.

> In Ephesians 5:33, the writer Paul gives some great marriage
> advice when he says, "Each one of you also must love his wife as
> he loves himself, and the wife must respect her husband."

Now there is nothing wrong with the man respecting his wife and the wife loving her husband. There is just something extra special for a husband when he hears from his wife, "Baby, I respect you. You are the man! I appreciate how much you provide and protect us." And there is just something extra special when a wife hears from her husband, "Baby, I love you! I cannot be without you. You are all I think about when I get up in the morning and when I go to bed at night." The man craves respect, and the woman yearns for love. When love and respect are given, it addresses their number one fear. The husband does not have to worry about being a failure when his wife respects him for trying and never giving up, and when she believes in him even when he does not. The wife does not have to be afraid of abandonment when her husband regularly tells her and shows her how much he loves her and desires to be with her. He's not going anywhere; in fact, his love reveals he cannot be without her. Through love and respect, the husband and wife can connect on a whole new level. And that is another great reason God created marriage.

> Genesis 2:24 says, "That is why the man leaves his father and mother and is united to his wife, and they become one flesh."

Let's break down this verse, because it gives us some of the key elements to what makes marriage, well…marriage. One important element: the man is able to leave his father and mother. He is at a point in his life where he does not have to live in his parents' basement or mooch off of their groceries. Not only can he take care of himself, but he is in a position to take care of someone else, his bride-to-be. Back in the first century, if a Jewish young man wanted to marry a Jewish young lady, he would offer her a cup of wine as a marriage proposal. If she drank from his glass of wine, she was accepting his proposal and pledged to be married to this man. They would agree to not drink wine together again until the day of their wedding feast. Then the young man would leave. He would go off to prepare and often build a home for his new family. Sometimes this new home was an addition built onto his father's house. Within the new home, the man would need to build a new bedroom for him and his bride-to-be, and often he would build their future bed. Once all these projects were complete, the young man had proven he could provide for his new family, a family of his own. He would show up to his fiancé, informing her of the provisions prepared for their new family. There would then be a wedding, a feast and a lot of wine.

If you ever go to a Jewish wedding celebration, there is a point in the celebration where the family of the bride breaks a glass and yells out, "Mazel tov!" The phrase is an expression meaning "Good luck!" or "We wish you well!" The breaking of the glass symbolizes the breaking away of the bride from her existing family to be joined to her new family. It is as if her family is saying, we have cared for her and provided for her up until this point in her life, and now it is the groom's turn. It is also acknowledging the bride has been an active contributor to her own family, and now she will contribute, nurture, and manage a new family with her groom. And so, they wish them well as they are now independent of their own families and prepared to provide and take care of each other together as a new family. This is a key part of marriage.

Another key part of marriage revealed in the scripture: the man is "united with his wife." The husband and wife are to connect in a way that substitutes for some of the previous roles of their parents. This does not mean they are no longer sons and daughters; it does, however, mean they will become the human care providers for each other.

The third key part of the marriage verse: "they become one flesh." This is both metaphorical and physical. Yes, there is the unity of being together emotionally, intellectually, and spiritually, but this verse is also about being together sexually. Sex is a big part of marriage. God knows this because He created sex for marriage. We may get uncomfortable about the subject, but God does not shy away from the topic. Sex in marriage is another way the husband and wife can become deeply connected to one another. God even set up our brains so that through sex, we would become more connected to each other in thought and emotions. Through chemicals like dopamine and epinephrine, the brain burns deep memories and neurological connections to each other during the act of sex. Also, during the act of sex, the body releases chemicals like oxytocin. This is a bonding chemical. It is the same chemical released within the woman after childbirth. It is why a woman wants to hold her baby after it has been delivered even though the baby had previously caused her much pain. She wants to be close to the baby, to feel skin-on-skin. That same chemical is released in the body of the man and woman during sex. It only creates a desire and a feeling of closeness, deep connectedness. Another chemical released within the body during the act of sex is serotonin. Studies show this chemical is released in high amounts during sex with your spouse. It is the chemical that lets your brain know you did a good thing, and now you are fully satisfied. Sex is a healthy way for the husband and wife to become more and more connected to each other on multiple levels.

4 God created marriage to provide a nurturing and loving family for children.

It does not matter if you don't have children yet, or if you are creating a blended family, it is important to understand that God loves children. He loves them so much that He had them in mind when He created marriage.

Genesis 1:28 says, "God blessed them and said to them,
'Be fruitful and increase in number, fill the earth...'"

Right after God creates man and woman and unites them together through marriage, God tells them to go make babies. Why? Because a healthy marriage is the base for a healthy family.

There was a study represented in the Harvard Business Review that shared, employees who take eleven or more of their vacation days per year were thirty percent more likely to receive a raise. Wait, what? Isn't it supposed to be the employees who spend all waking hours at work that should be getting the raises? Well, the math does not quite work that way. Why? Because the employees taking time for vacation are typically spending those vacation days with their spouses and kids. As a result of more time spent with family, the employees return to work filled and skilled.

They are filled because life is about sharing the most important moments with the most important people. We feel good when we spend quality time with our spouse and kids; we feel like we did something good and meaningful. When we return to work feeling good, we tend to do good work. There are studies revealing people who feel positive about life are 20 to 30% more productive at work. They are about 40% better at sales. People who spend quality time with their family come to work filled up with all sorts of positive energy.

People who spend quality time with their families also show up to their workplace more skilled. This is because the most important skills in life are built, tested, and reinforced within the marriage and parenting relationships. If you want to build communication skills, go on a getaway with your spouse. If you want to strengthen your skill of patience, visit your in-laws. If you want to increase the development of your leadership and management skills, go on a family vacation. Spend quality time with family and watch your skills increase. If you can plan and manage a family picnic with toddlers, you can manage a major project with multiple moving pieces at work. If you can work through family-in-law traditions and conversations that seem foreign to the way you grew up, you can understand and land a complicated business deal. If you can learn how to deal with a spouse who has a rough month, you can easily deal with a coworker having a bad day. People who value, plan, and spend quality time with their family, come to work highly skilled. You could easily argue the best thing you could do for your job is to prioritize your family even more.

Guess what? The best thing you can do for your family is to prioritize marriage even more. If you ever hear a married couple explaining their life with the statement, "It is all about the children," that marriage is in trouble. Studies show kids thrive in a home with a healthy marriage. You would be doing your kids a disservice to value them as more important than your spouse. One of the best gifts you can give your children is to model what it looks like to place your spouse as the most important of all human relationships. Chances are they will get married someday, and for better or worse, their parents will be the biggest influence on their life and future marriage. The best gift you can give your sons and daughters is a clear picture of what it looks like for a husband to love and cherish his wife, and a wife to respect and cheer on her husband. The love and loyalty they observe is most likely what they will invest in their own marriage someday. This prioritization never backfires. You never hear a kid complaining that his dad loves his mom too much, or that her mom treats her dad with such appreciation. When you prioritize the marriage over the children, you end up loving and caring for the children even more than if you were to prioritize them first.

Before we move onto the next reason God created marriage, it is important to understand that the best thing you can do for your marriage is to prioritize Jesus above your marriage. There are all sorts of studies revealing Christian married couples have more satisfying sex lives, and couples who pray together statistically stay together. Why? Because when Jesus is guiding your decision-making process, He will guide you to always love, respect, forgive, and value each other.

So, in recap, the best thing you can do for your job is to love your family even more. The best thing you can do for your family is to love your spouse even more. The best thing you can do for your marriage is to love Jesus even more.

Here is the sad reality. When you get these out of order, it begins to affect your relationships in this same order. If you start prioritizing work over all the others, it will first affect your relationship with God, then with your spouse, then your kids, and eventually work will be wondering why you are drained and producing less. The good news is if you get any of these out of order, you can always run back to Jesus, and He will help you get the rest back into order.

Sometimes we find ourselves living Plan B, C, or D in life because, for some reason or another, Plan A was never followed. While God can do some great work through Plan B, C, or even D, God's Plan A produces the best results with the least amount of conflict or turbulence. God's Plan A for a healthy family is a man and a woman married for life pouring into their children. This allows for godly offspring. This allows for a loving and nurturing environment. This allows for a great family, and great families often change this world for the better.

5 God created marriage with the intention that a couple would be able to contribute.

I don't believe that it would be hard for me to sell you on the idea there is a purpose for your life. You are unique and loaded with potential. There is something bigger for you to contribute to, as an individual in this world. That is all true. Do you know what else is true? There is a purpose for your marriage.

Yes, you chose each other, but I wonder how much of it actually felt like a choice. Many couples describe falling in love as the realization they could not imagine being without each other. They were compelled by love, meaning they fell in love. Well, God claims to be the very definition of love in 1 John 4:8. In other words, love does not define God. Rather God defines love. When you experience love, you are learning more about God. When love seems to drive you together, then it is God who is actually leading you to each other. If God brought you together, then He must have done it for a reason. There is a purpose behind it. God has a purpose for your marriage.

This purpose goes beyond your wedding day. It is bigger than you as a couple. It is a purpose that ties you both to something bigger going on in our world. It is a way you can contribute to this world for good, much more effectively than if you were not a couple. God didn't do addition when He brought you together; He did multiplication.

He combined different skills, talents, perspectives, giftings, resources from two unique people that, when placed together, enhance each other to do something big, something important. No other creatures are given this kind of purpose and mission.

> Genesis 1:26 says, "Then God said, 'Let us make mankind in our
> image, in our likeness, so that they may rule over the fish in the sea
> and the birds in the sky, over the livestock and all the wild animals,
> and over all the creatures that move along the ground."

God gave men and women a purpose, a mission. It is bigger and more important than any other piece of His creation. There is a mission for your marriage. There is a way you can contribute together, better than you could apart. The two of you together can make a better product. Start thinking about and exploring what that mission might be. How can you contribute as a couple to the good in this world? How can your marriage leave a lasting impression that changes the lives of everyone else on this planet for the better? How can you not just plan a wedding day, but start planning a marriage mission?

Sometimes these explorations and communication can feel like awkward conversations. Let me let you in on a little secret. The best marriages are filled with awkward conversations. That is part of what makes marriage so interesting. And God has an adventure for every couple.

If you don't have a mission bigger than yourselves, you will get bored. If all the arrows in your life point inward to make it all about you, then your marriage will find trouble fast. But if you can start looking out beyond yourself, then something exciting and meaningful awaits.

Your marriage is important to God. In fact, God starts the Bible with a wedding story between a man and a woman in the presence of God. And God ends the Bible with a wedding story. It is a big wedding story that involves the whole of the universe. It is a wedding between God and His people through victory found in Jesus.

You will have to ask God, pray, and maybe even fast to find out what your bigger marriage mission is. God has a purpose for your marriage, and if you want to understand your God-given purpose more clearly, then you will need to get to know the God who gave it to you. There is an adventure waiting for you that goes beyond your wedding day. Are you ready to see what awaits?

HINTS, TIPS, AND TRICKS

Welcome to the life-changing adventure that is *Mentor Us*. Before you get started, here are some tips on how to best use this tool. That's right, *Mentor Us* is a tool. This means that the tool should never trump the users, but rather the users should always trump the tool. Use *Mentor Us* in ways that best meet the Mentor and Mentees needs. If you don't like a question, then don't use it. If you have a better way to describe something, than use your definition. If you want to change the order, skip a part, spend more time on one area, add or take away some homework, then do it. You won't hurt our feelings. We just want to help get a mentoring relationship started and equip couples for marriage.

TIP 1   Get at least one book for the Mentor couple to use and one separate book for the Mentee couple. This way, both couples can take a book home, read ahead or review the material, and keep notes and answers that are pertinent to each couple. For the best possible results, we suggest one book per person. This allows the book to act more like a personal journal and less like a workbook. It will likely yield more intimate and honest written answers. You can always compare and share the answers you desire with the other participants at appropriate times.

TIP 2   Read ahead and answer questions on your own time before your mentoring sessions. Not everyone can come up with a great answer or thought when put on the spot. Some participants would rather answer the questions ahead of time so they can spend the majority of the session time sharing the answers they have already thought through. Taking time to process beforehand is helpful to everyone. Read the material so you know what you are going to talk about before you talk about it. There will not be enough time to talk about every little detail packed within this book during your mentorship sessions. Reading ahead will make sure you are prepared to discuss what is important to you.

TIP 3   Ask lots of questions. Yes, we have loaded this material with questions, because that is how we often learn best. Jesus frequently taught His followers by asking questions, and it got them thinking. If one written question spurs on another unwritten question, ask it. Tangents are okay with us. Let the conversation go where it must. We trust you to get it back on track when the time is right. Also, we would especially encourage the Mentees to prepare questions outside of the material for their Mentors to answer. This ensures that the vast wealth of knowledge available from the Mentor couple to the Mentee couple is not hindered by questions we forgot to ask in the material.

TIP 4   Use the blank lines under the questions to fill in your own answers, but also feel free to use them to write some of the other participants' answers. This can especially help the Mentor couple remember details occurring in the Mentee couple's life. You can also use the space to jot down notes, thoughts, and questions for future reference.

TIP 5   Start and end each session by allowing each individual to share what is currently in their head and on their heart. For example, we think it is always important to take a moment and see how each individual is doing. A lot can happen between sessions, and it is good to talk about it and gauge the mood of each participant before you move forward. We would also strongly suggest that you reserve time to answer questions that are not in the material, but still important to the participant. We encourage you to use the prayer time built into each session and write down prayer requests. It is always amazing to see God at work, but sometimes you can miss it if you don't write it down.

TIP 6   Enjoy the moments. We know that not all mentorships last a lifetime. In fact, most mentorships last a season (and that is okay). So, enjoy the season. Learn as much as you can and enjoy the time that you have together. As you grow, it is okay, and often necessary, to change things up. This mentorship will help identify future paths for further growth. Everything great has a starting point and often an ending point. Think of your growth plan as seasons and steps rather than a locked-in path. Measure and take each step and let God guide the rest. Enjoy the journey!

GROWTH OPPORTUNITIES ANALYSIS

Mentor Us is intentionally packed with questions, lessons, and information to equip you for marriage. Because every person and marriage is different, some sections of the material may be more valuable to your marriage than others, thus demanding more attention and consideration. In order to better navigate which sections of the material to require more focus for your marriage, we recommend using a Growth Opportunities Analysis (GOA) tool.

This GOA, or tools like it, are simple tests to be taken by the Mentees as individuals before your first session together. The results from the test will help identify opportunities for growth within the Mentee's marriage. It will also serve as a guide for the Mentors as they make preparations to focus on key skill areas of marriage, which can overall benefit the Mentee couple.

Our Story

CHAPTER ONE

HOW'S IT GOING?

You made it to your first meeting! Let's start by answering some questions.

What would you hope to get out of these mentoring sessions? (If you don't want to answer this question now, think about it and we can come back to answer it at the end of the session.)

_____

_____

What do you think will be different about your relationship and circumstances after your wedding day?

_____

_____

For our first session together the focus will be on our story.

"The telling and hearing of stories is a bonding ritual that breaks through illusions of separateness and activates a deep sense of our collective interdependence."

Annette Simmons

MY STORY

Everyone has a story. And every story is important. Within these stories we find a window into the life of another person. We discover their traditions, values, family dynamics, faith background, relationships, and experiences that have formed this person into who they are today. Our past is important; it helps us understand and connect to others in ways we may have never expected.

Our stories connect the past and present to the future and they connect and become a part of YOUR story together.

The mentorship journey is all about moving forward, but if you want to move forward with someone then you need to know where they came from. In order to look ahead, we must first look backwards.

Do you remember your friends from kindergarten and elementary school? Depending on where you lived, they may have rode the bus home with you or you might have all walked home together after school. At that age, you didn't have to know a lot about someone to be their friend – playing in the backyard or producing puppet shows was enough of a common ground for relationships to blossom. But there were those times, usually when a group of friends stayed for dinner or spent the night at your house, when it became clear that your friends have a different story than you.

Imagine this scenario: a seven-year-old boy lives at home with his mother and father and one night he invites 5 of his friends over for dinner and to spend the night. Over the course of that night and morning you would hear the parents say, "well in our house we don't use that kind of language... in our house we always wash our hands before we eat... in our house we go to bed before midnight." And you would hear the kids say things like, "well in my house we can have snacks whenever we want... well in my house we are allowed to watch that channel... well in my house we have to go to bed early and then go to church in the morning."

The deeper a relationship grows the more we uncover parts of each other's life story. You begin to realize that not every family is just like yours, not everyone has had the same experiences or expectations in their life. That is why it is so important for you to know your story...so that you can begin to envision what your marriage should- or shouldn't-look like. Be very intentional about what parts of your story you want to be a part of your marriage future!

So, let's get started Telling Your Story.

If you don't feel like a great storyteller, don't worry too much about this one; no one knows your story better than you do. So let's give it a try. Take turns sharing the answers to the following questions:

FAMILY

What was your family like growing up?

The before & after EBV

What role does your family play in your life today?

social, spiritual, fiancial, wisdom

How do you get along with your future in-laws?

great! & tbd

Do you have any family members or friends who have a strong influence over
your upcoming marriage? If so, explain.

parents

FOUNDATION

What values did you grow up with in your home? (Family first, education is most important, better to be nice than honest, etc.)

kind, honest, considerat, rules, Christ, education

What traditions did you grow up with in your home? (Holiday celebrations, dinner table seating, annual family trips, etc.)

Pre/post EBV, x-mas gifts, alternating holidays, rest/individual time

"The beginning of a friendship, the fact that two people out of thousands around them can meet and connect and become friends, seems like a kind of magic to me. But maintaining a friendship requires work. I don't mean that as a bad thing. Good art requires work as well."
Charles de Lint

FRIENDSHIP

When did you and your partner first meet?

volleyball 2020

Who are some of your closest friends and what role do they play in your life?

Caitlin, Christopher, Lindsey, mom, Shelby, V&A

Why did you choose the people in your wedding party?

family, whitness, support, love

Do you have any 'couple' friends? If so, explain.

L&R, E&J, V&N

FAITH BACKGROUND

Growing up, what role did faith play in your life?

knowledge, relationship, prayer, P/PEBV

How has your faith background impacted your life?

direction, decisions, comfort, plans

"Every great love starts with a great story..."
Nicholas Sparks

FINANCIAL SITUATION

What kind of conversations have you had about finances? Do you plan to merge your accounts after the wedding?

spreadsheets logistics values, priorities, responsibility
yes

Throughout your life, what were you taught about the value of money?

important but not everything

Are you more of a spender or a saver?

both/saver/spender

OUR STORY

Sharing your individual story is a building block to a strong and healthy marriage mentorship. Think of all the different pieces of your past that have dramatically impacted your present day life. Those real experiences are tools; they are mentorship currency, and when shared in the telling of your story they will create personal opportunities for growth, encouragement, and empathy.

By sharing your story you are building a connection and an understanding; you are learning more than just where and who someone is, you are seeing where they have come from and how they have gotten here. And, most importantly, you are able to better work together in determining where you want to go from here. This is especially true for a couple preparing for marriage.

Forming a marriage is similar to the forming of a child; the DNA of two people – their family history, genetic make up, physical design, and chemical dependencies – unite together to create a new life. This new life is a new story, formed out of two other stories. The child is new and separate from the parents; however, it still never loses the DNA of the two people that made it. In the same way, marriage is the welding of two stories into one new story – your new story cannot be made without submitting your old story to each other.

There is a beautiful design in the DNA of marriage. In the Bible, we find this statement on marriage and the coming together of two people:

"Then the Lord God made a woman from the rib he had taken out of the man, and he brought her to the man. The man said, 'This is now bone of my bones and flesh of my flesh; she shall be called 'woman,' for she was taken out of man.' That is why a man leaves his father and mother and is united to his wife, and they become one flesh. Adam and his wife were both naked, and they felt no shame."   —Genesis 2:22-25

Two people, two lives, two stories, become one life, one united story. As we approach marriage, we are preparing our hearts and minds to be united together with a person whom we deeply love. At this point, you will belong to each other and, therefore, your stories will belong to each other.

There is a temptation to view marriage as two people being cut in half and then giving their half to their spouse to create a "whole" person. The problem with that idea is you are only giving half of yourself! The union of marriage is designed to be one's whole self, no holding back – and in return you receive all of someone else, all of their story becomes yours. In the passage from Genesis, the man and wife were able to give each other all of themselves, their most vulnerable and naked selves, and feel no shame. So there is no reason to hold back part of your story from your spouse. **God created marriage so a man and women would experience companionship.** He does not want us to feel alone. The incredible reality of human life is we need to be with people, to connect together, and to have companionship. We need to be known, and we need to know others. We need to feel love and a sense of belonging. God uses marriage to help satisfy an internal need for belonging. When we make our vows and commit to our spouse we are declaring we belong to each other in the past, present, and the future. At that point, two stories forever become one and a new chapter of our story will be written together.

HELP   Sometimes there are parts of our story we don't like that cause us great pain or embarrassment. We may try to convince ourselves these parts of our story are not important or they no longer matter. It is in the telling of these parts of our story we learn to become vulnerable with one another and can feel accepted and validated by this process. Having a great marriage relationship requires building a safe environment to share anything with our spouse in order to be encouraged and supported. Some of these stories might require help digging them out in order to share. This is where a counselor might be able to help. Consider whether there are any parts of your story that might need some help processing and sharing. Look for next steps where you can involve a professional who can help.

WHERE DO WE GO WITH THIS?

Sharing life and telling your story is an ongoing process. In mentorship, we will share our stories together with the goal of encouraging one another, gaining wisdom, and celebrating life together.

We all need to commit to two continual actions: share your individual stories with each other, and in your marriage be unified to tell one great couple's story together. Planning a beautiful wedding is a wonderful goal, but it isn't as important as committing to planning a great marriage story together.

Mentors, this is a great time for you to share a little bit of your story and what you hope to gain through this experience. Mentees, let's answer a couple more questions.

REFLECTION

What do you want the first chapter of your story as a couple to look like?

worship creator, humility

Are there potential areas in your marriage that will make unity difficult?
Explain.

gender?

If you did not get to answer this question before, what to do you hope to get out of these mentoring sessions?

clarity, humility, hope, plans

HOW DO WE MOVE FORWARD?

HOMEWORK

Moving forward in preparation for our next session together we want to take time to do personality assessments. Personality assessments are great tools to bring clarity to our strength and growth areas, traits, and how we approach and solve life issues. It will also help you to create a better marriage dialogue as you begin to define YOUR story.

Some great personality assessment tools to use are:

_____

_____

(Examples: Wired that Way, Enneagram, DiSC Profile, Myers-Briggs Type Indicator)

Please complete your personality test prior to our next meeting. It will help us determine your nature and how the two of you will work together to complement one another.

CLOSING PRAYER

Before we depart let's close in prayer. Do you have any prayer requests?

_____

_____

A GOOD SUGGESTION

Between now and your next session, read through the following chapter and fill in as many answers as possible.

Our Design

CHAPTER TWO

HOW'S IT GOING?

Welcome to the second session! After doing your homework, hopefully you have received some clarity or new understanding about yourself. Let's start our session together by answering a few questions:

Is there anything else you would like to share regarding your story that you did not get to share last session? Or any questions you did not get to ask?

_____

_____

We will discuss the results of your homework from last session a little bit later in this session. While working on the personality test, was there anything you found surprising or confusing?

_____

_____

What have you been learning about yourself?

_____

_____

For our second session together, the focus will be on our design.

MY DESIGN

In this session, we are going to examine your composition, or profile. But this won't be a conversation about what you look like or needing to go to the gym. We are actually talking about our internal design—the tangible qualities of our heart, soul, and mind. So let's talk about our DESIGN:

DESIRES
The dreams and passions that drive your life.

EXPERIENCE
The knowledge formed from your past interactions and observations.

STRESSORS
That which triggers stress and how you handle it.

IDEALS
The values and beliefs that influence the choices you make and teach.

GIFTS
Natural and developed talents and abilities.

NATURE
Your pre-wired personality and character traits that determine how you best operate.

These six key components help identify who you and your partner really are and how you impact the world around you. Most people have a general feeling of what their DESIGN is like, but many have not taken the time to clearly define these parts of themselves or discover them in others.

Take the time now to answer questions regarding you and your partner's DESIGN:

"Design is not just what it looks like and what it feels like. Design is how it works."

Steve Jobs

DESIRES

These are the desires of your heart, the passions that inspire and unveil future destinations for our work, family, health, and faith.

What do you get most excited about? What gets your blood pumping? What are you passionate about? What would you love to do more often if you were able?

_____

_____

What do you want to accomplish, achieve, or create in the next 5 to 10 years?

_____

_____

EXPERIENCE

These are monumental events, whether good or bad, that made a lasting impact in our design and on our lives.

Make a list of your top three positive life experiences and then your top three negative experiences that have shaped your life:

Positive   Negative

_____   _____

_____   _____

_____   _____

* Note that some negative experiences have hurt us so deeply that it is worth working on them with a professional in order to bring about proper healing.

STRESSORS

These are the unique worries, pressures, and irritants that trigger stress in our life, as well as the way in which we react and handle these particular aggravations.

In one column answer the question of, "What troubles, worries, pressures, and irritants stress each of you out the most?" In the other column answer the question of: "When you are stressed how do you typically react?"

We will have the opportunity to explore some of the specifics of your stressors later in this session. For now, please complete this exercise:

What stresses you out?   How do you react to these stresses?

_____   _____

_____   _____

_____   _____

IDEALS

These are the philosophies that drive how we behave and our expectation of how we think others should behave.

What is most important to you? What beliefs or values do you have that are unwavering?

_____

_____

When you look at the world around you, what breaks your heart or makes you angry?

_____

_____

What do you expect of yourselves in your work, home, and marriage?

_____

_____

What do you expect of your partner in your work, home, and marriage?

_____

_____

GIFTS

These are talents, skills, abilities, and strengths that may come natural to you or that you have developed over time.

What do you think are some of your top gifts that seem to come naturally to you?

_____

_____

What do you think are some of your top skills that you have built over time?

_____

_____

NATURE

There are essential features to your personality, character traits that are as much of a part of you as your skin.

According to the Personality Profile test you both took, what type of personality, or mixture of personalities are you? Do you agree with the results?

_____

_____

Choose two strengths and one weakness in your main personality trait that rings true about you. How will this impact your relationship with your spouse? (How do your personalities complement one another? How might your personalities cause conflict with each other?)

_____

_____

WHY IS MY DESIGN IMPORTANT?

Similar to your story, your design plays a huge role in this mentorship and marriage. Where your story is the vehicle, your design is the fuel. Think of it this way: your story answers the "what," "where," and "when" questions of someone's life, your design answers the "how" and the "why." Ultimately, you need both of these elements together to truly know "who" a person is.

Discovering and sharing our design with those around us allows for a deeper, truer connection. Consider this passage from the Bible:

> "Just as a body, though one, has many parts, but all its many parts form one body, so it is with Christ. For we were all baptized by one Spirit so as to form one body—whether Jews or Gentiles, slave or free—and we were all given the one Spirit to drink. Even so the body is not made up of one part but of many. Now if the foot should say, 'Because I am not a hand, I do not belong to the body,' it would not for that reason stop being part of the body. And if the ear should say, 'Because I am not an eye, I do not belong to the body,' it would not for that reason stop being part of the body. If the whole body were an eye, where would the sense of hearing be? If the whole body were an ear, where would the sense of smell be? But in fact God has placed the parts in the body, every one of them, just as he wanted them to be."   —1 Corinthians 12:12-18

This passage from the Bible illustrates that different designs serve different, complementary functions. There is no sense in competing or comparing your design against someone else's, only you have the ability to do what you are designed for. Our unique design brings unique utility and weakness. The design of marriage is to unite us together in love, multiplying our strengths and supporting each other's weaknesses. You will never be stronger on your own; you were not designed that way.

Statistically we marry our opposites. Our friends and co-workers we hang out with tend to be more like ourselves. Our buddies and girlfriends are usually wired similar to us, but our spouse is usually the opposite. This is ironic since so many dating sites focus on similarities and common interests. In the beginning of the relationship we respect and admire the differences, but as time goes on we tend to resent and get annoyed by the differences. To make matters worse, we go to our friends to weigh in on the differences and they side with us because they're wired the same as us.

So why are we attracted to our opposites? **God created marriage for a couple to complement each other.** While God is the only one who can truly complete us, He uses marriage to help complement and compensate for us. He provides someone who is strong in some areas where we are weak. God always, through a relationship with Himself and with your partner and others, wants to continually move us from weak to more complete.

> In Genesis 2:18 it says, "The Lord God said, 'It is not good for the man to be alone. I will make a helper suitable for him.'"

The word helper is not a subservient term like an assistant or sidekick. In the original Hebrew language of which this text was written, it means someone who is strong where the other person is weak. God uses the word in later scripture to describe Himself. The "helper" is a missing part. It is that other person with a different DESIGN that complements us in ways God knows we need.

WHERE DO WE GO WITH THIS?

Knowing your design as a couple helps you see where your combined strengths and weaknesses are. Without knowing the design, you will not be able to capitalize on your strengths or identify your opportunities for growth.

Let's first take some time to review the Growth Opportunities Analysis results you completed prior to the first session. We are going to use this assessment as a guide. We will use the discovered growth opportunities to help determine where to spend more time in our learning and time together. It may not be a perfect guide, so feel free to emphasize a subject or spend more time on a section you feel may need more emphasis. You can always interrupt if you want to cover more. Let's start by generally reviewing the results of the analysis.

MENTEES

After reviewing the results of your Growth Opportunities Analysis, what are your initial thoughts?

_____

_____

Which growth opportunities excite you the most? Why?

_____

_____

MENTORS

Where have you grown the most since your wedding? Are there still opportunities for growth in your marriage, in which you are interested?

_____

_____

In your experience, what methods helped you to grow the most?

_____

_____

KEY AREAS

Let's explore three key areas of opportunity for a healthy marriage.

Mentors focus on one or two based on the Growth Opportunities Analysis. The Let's Talk and Let's Kick it Up a Notch sections are designed for deeper digging into a skill or topic. Choose which sections to complete based on need and your own discretion.

1 OUR PERSONALITIES

2 OUR ROLES

3 OUR STRESSORS

OUR PERSONALITIES: LET'S LEARN

Everyone has a personality, and putting two personalities together is truly an adventure. In some moments, there is an incredible understanding and appreciation for how we think and act; in other moments, sudden frustration or confusion springs up and creates momentary road block. For most couples, partners have different and opposite personality types. Learning more about yourself and your partner's personality allows you to see how you will complement each other and anticipate where you may get tripped up.

OUR PERSONALITIES: LET'S TRY

Looking back, your personality types are traceable all throughout your relationship together. From the time you first met, to the day that you got engaged, your personalities shine throughout your story as a couple. Let's try this:

One at a time, retell the story of how you fell in love. Try to share some examples of how your partner's personality attracted you to them.

_____

_____

What part of their personality grabbed your attention and affection the most?

_____

_____

OUR PERSONALITIES: LET'S TALK

Take a moment to compare and contrast the unique parts of your two personalities.

What habits and/or characteristics does you partner have that you really admire?

_____

_____

What habits and/or characteristics does your partner have that frustrate you? How do you react to these frustrations?

_____

_____

How often do you think the differences in your personalities will create conflict in your future marriage?

_____

_____

Do your individual personalities match up well with the role and responsibilities you have taken in your relationship together? Why or why not?

_____

_____

OUR PERSONALITIES: LET'S KICK IT UP A NOTCH

Share a few examples of how your personality differences strengthen and complement each other. Write down how you think this will benefit the further success of your marriage.

Your partner's personality is part of what drew your heart towards them, so how can you intentionally appreciate their personality instead of trying to make it more like yours? Share your thoughts with each other.

_____

_____

OUR ROLES: LET'S LEARN

One of the great gifts of marriage is companionship, the gift of a lifelong partner and teammate. Through the bonds of your relationship, you are never alone. The gift of a teammate is made even greater with a healthy understanding of each other's role and responsibility. With trust and teamwork, you can each contribute and uniquely strengthen your family.

It is normal for both partners to enter a marriage relationship with preconceived ideas about roles and responsibilities. We often look back to our own parents and friends as examples for what a husband or wife should do or how they should interact. However, it is important to intentionally evaluate and establish roles and responsibilities that will best fit you, not your parents or the families on television. By lining up your roles and responsibilities to match your personalities and gifts, you are creating a healthier and more satisfying partnership for your team.

OUR ROLES: LET'S TRY

Imagine creating a game plan for your household, a set of plays and positions that you'd like to see your team put into practice. Make two lists: first, come up with four roles/responsibilities for yourself to do for your household; second, come up with four roles/responsibilities that you would like to see your partner do.

Roles for Me:

cleaning
cooking / groceries
emotional support
family trips / friend outings

Roles for My Spouse:

Primary income
car maintenace
emotional support
Biblical leadership,

OUR ROLES: LET'S TALK

Once you've come up with your lists, take a moment to compare what you came up with.

Were you surprised by anything that was or wasn't written?

_no_

Would you say the lists are based on personalities and gifts or more focused on preconceived thoughts, traditional gender roles, or something else?

preferences, gifting, scripture

Now that you have seen each other's lists, try to combine them together and create a new list with 4 roles/responsibilities for each of you that you can both agree on.

Agreed Upon Roles for Him:

_____

_____

_____

_____

Agreed Upon Roles for Her:

_____

_____

_____

_____

If this is proving to be a difficult task, don't give up! You can come back to this another time and continue ironing this out. Your Mentors can share more about their experiences defining roles and responsibilities and how their expectations have shifted throughout their marriage. It is important to consider that different seasons of life may change some of the roles and responsibilities, you may grow in new areas and new responsibilities might arise. This is an ongoing process that will require patience and flexibility from the whole team.

OUR ROLES: LET'S KICK IT UP A NOTCH

There are probably some activities that you both naturally do more than the other person: drive, cook, plan dates, do dishes, shop for groceries, etc. Take some time this week to take note of the things that are predominantly done by one person. If you want an extra challenge, take a day or two and switch up who does some of those one-sided tasks. Afterwards, share your thoughts and feelings about doing the roles/activities you don't normally do and share how it felt watching your partner do the roles/activities that you normally do.

OUR STRESSORS: LET'S LEARN

Stress comes in various forms, often at times when its least expected or welcome, and that is what makes it stressful! We usually associate stress with bad news, but the best things in life bring stress: having a baby, moving into a new house, getting a new job, and getting married. With the abundance of stress in our lives, its important to understand how each of us reacts and manages our stressors.

OUR STRESSORS: LET'S TRY

Take time to each answer and identify stressors:

WHEN are you most stressed? What times of the year, month, or week are you most stressed (ex. For an Accountant, Tax Season)?

heavy work load, poor diet, less sleep

WHERE are you most stressed (ex. At home, work, school, parent's house, on the road, etc.)?

WHO is around you when you are most stressed (ex. Parents, kids, boss, co-workers, clients, etc.)?

_____

_____

WHAT are you doing when you feel most stressed (ex. Driving, working with money, cleaning, competing, trying to manage, etc.)?

_____

_____

WHY do you think you are sometimes susceptible to stress (ex. Tired, busy, feel out of balanced, old wounds ect.)?

_____

_____

OUR STRESSORS: LET'S TALK

Did any of your stressors stick out or surprise you both? If so, how do you currently feel about that stressor?

_____

_____

What are some ways that you currently deal with stress in your life?

_____

_____

Can you think of a reasonable way that your partner could help you deal with stress, particularly the heavier stressors you currently experience?

_____

_____

What other steps could you both take together to help manage and lessen stress?

_____

_____

OUR STRESSORS: LET'S KICK IT UP A NOTCH

The wedding is coming up and we all know that there will be stressful parts in planning, communicating, and maybe even on the day of your wedding. Take some time to go through this Wedding Stressor exercise. It will help you share your vision for how things will go and give you the chance to preemptively come to a compromise if necessary.

HELPFUL HINTS:

- Listen to understand before proposing solutions

- Choose the best time and place to talk about difficult matters

- Consider whether deeper issues are underlying your conflict

WEDDING STRESSORS EXERCISE

Personal preferences, opposing opinions and disagreement over differences can cause stress during the wedding planning process. As you complete this worksheet, notice where your visions for the wedding match up and areas where compromise can be reached.

Make a note if you want to revisit a section (especially areas where compromise cannot be reached) during your next mentorship session.

	HER VISION	HIS VISION	COMPROMISE
Venue`	_____	_____	_____
	_____	_____	_____
Date/Time	_____	_____	_____
	_____	_____	_____
Guest List	_____	_____	_____
	_____	_____	_____
Task Division	_____	_____	_____
	_____	_____	_____
Family Roles	_____	_____	_____
	_____	_____	_____
Traditions	_____	_____	_____
	_____	_____	_____

HOW DO WE MOVE FORWARD?

HOMEWORK

Moving forward in preparation for our next session together we want to take time to do the Love Language Assessment. This will give some good communication information and prepare us for the next time we meet and discuss our love life.

Love Language Assessment: *www.5lovelanguages.com/profile/couples/*

CLOSING PRAYER

Before we depart let's close in prayer. Do you have any prayer requests?

_____

_____

A GOOD SUGGESTION

Between now and your next session, read through the following chapter and fill in as many answers as possible.

Our Communication

CHAPTER THREE

HOW'S IT GOING?

Welcome to the third session of *Mentor Us*! Thank you for your commitment and openness as we talked through these first couple of sessions. There are still many important conversations ahead of us. Before we begin this session, let's start by answering a few questions:

Is there anything else you would like to share regarding your design that you did not get to share last session? Or any questions you did not get to ask?

_____

_____

What have you been learning about yourself?

_____

_____

What did you learn from your 5 Love Languages homework? What is your primary love language?

_____

_____

Can you think of a time you have seen your partner's primary love language reveal itself? If so, explain.

_____

_____

Being in love is one component for a strong marriage but in order for that marriage relationship to grow and mature, we need other vital components, like good communication skills.

For our third session together the focus will be on our communication.

COMMUNICATION

Communication is the expression and demonstration of information. Most people believe they are great communicators, yet studies show this is by far the greatest struggle for couples in marriage. Perhaps this is because many people fall short of understanding what healthy and effective communication really looks like. Effective communication is not about how many words you say or how loud your voice gets. Healthy communication is not issuing demands, making accusations, or retaliating in anger. Miscommunication causes hostility, discord, or division. It destroys your ability to resolve conflict inside and around your marriage. Talking, in and of itself is easy. True communication is difficult because it requires more than one person to hear and understand what is being communicated. There are many subtle things that disrupt our ability to communicate; the greatest examples are found in our body language and tone of voice. How we say something will determine how the listener will receive it. How we listen will determine how well the speaker feels understood. A key element needed for good communication is empathy. The difference between sympathy and empathy: sympathy is demonstrating to your partner that you agree with them, while empathy is demonstrating to your partner that you understand. Agreeing is not a requirement for good communication, but understanding how your partner thinks and feels in the moment is. And in order to demonstrate that you truly understand your partner, it will require more than words, because, after all, communication is so much more than words.

As we investigate our own communication preferences and the preferences of our spouse, our marriage will become stronger and the communication more intimate. Then we can witness effective communication that brings clarity and understanding to our relationship. We can experience healthy communication that brings harmony and peace to our home.

HOW WE CONVEY A MESSAGE   Our non-verbal communication is powerful. Dr. Albert Mehrabian did a study revealing that when we want to communicate our attitude and feelings on a topic, our communication consists of three main parts: words, tone and body language. Of the three, body language (with 55%) influences the reception of the message much more than the other two. Tone of voice comes in second at 38%, and your words that were actually spoken were only a mere 7%.

Facial expressions, posture, gestures, eye movement, touch, and the use of space are all ways we communicate with our bodies to help each other understand what we think and how we feel.

"90% of all management problems are caused by miscommunication."

Dale Carnegie

- WHY IS COMMUNICATION IMPORTANT? -

If you have ever traveled to a community foreign to you (where people speak a different language, hold different customs and traditions) then you understand the challenges that come with communication barriers. Finding a bathroom, ordering food, or getting a ride to the airport while traveling can be a difficult experience. Many times, travelers and refugees feel extremely disconnected from their surroundings because they struggle to communicate with most of the people around them. Where there is poor communication there is chaos and resentment; conflicts are not resolved and spawn more conflicts. Communication barriers ultimately create a sense of frustration, confusion, and isolation between people. This occurs between nations, communities, people, and spouses. Couples who lack healthy and effective communication will experience similar frustration, confusion, and the inability to resolve conflicts.

It is important to recognize that communication barriers exist in marriage. When we assume, instead of listen, we often presume the worst about motives and intentions. Our tone and body language often says something completely different than the words that come out of our mouth. We are capable of purposefully neglecting and withholding opportunities to communicate love and belonging to our spouse, because of the resentment or distrust that has crept into our heart. It is tragic and heart-breaking when a marriage has lost itself in miscommunication. We hope that by acknowledging these real threats to our marriage, we can better prepare ourselves to face them head on.

> "The Lord God said, 'It is not good for the man to be alone.
> I will make a helper suitable for him.'"   —Genesis 2:18

God created marriage so the male and female would be deeply connected. This connection is intended to be more than physical. Through marriage we also connect spiritually, emotionally and intellectually. In order to continually connect we must understand one another and communicate in accordance with each other's continual needs.

> "However, each one of you also must love his wife as he loves himself,
> and the wife must respect her husband."   —Ephesians 5:33

Through the marriage relationship God moves us from the devastation of potential rejection to protection. God knows what we need to hear and feel. Women need to hear and feel their man communicating love. Men need to hear and feel their woman communicating respect. When we are talking to our spouse, we want to be completely open and honest about the way we feel and share what is in our heart while at the same time appealing to our spouse's heart.

Often we must learn to slow down, breathe, and take the time to think upon what we are about to communicate to each other so we can do it in a healthy way. When spouses communicate well with each other there is less frustration, more fulfillment and deeper connection.

WHY MARRIAGES FAIL   "YourTango.com" polled 100 mental health professionals about the leading factors in failed marriages. 65% of professionals polled indicated that "communication problems" were the number one factor, followed by an "inability to resolve conflict" with 43%.

WHERE DO WE GO WITH THIS?

A healthy marriage requires a strong commitment to building and maintaining healthy communication skills. The ideology of commitment and marriage in our society is not the same as it has always been. We must rediscover the passion and humility it takes to learn to speak another person's love language, to listen without judgment, and to sacrifice necessary time to work on our marriage. A great place to start is to make sure you and your spouse have a solid understanding of your own communication traits so you can share with each other. Consider these questions individually and then share them:

HAPPY MARRIAGE	UNHAPPY MARRIAGE
"Happily married couples tend to: (a) talk to each other more often, (b) are more sensitive to each other's feelings, and (c) use non-verbal communication more effectively."	"Dysfunctional communication is the most frequent and damaging problem in marriages."

What adjectives would you use to describe your communication styles? (i.e. aggressive, avoidant, anxious, overly detailed, lengthy, open book, angry, fearful, silent, withdrawing, concise, hesitant, don't know how, etc.)

_____

_____

How do you think the Love Languages play into your communication style?

_____

_____

What do you think good communication in marriage looks like? Consider using your parents as a good or bad example.

_____

_____

When is a time you think you both communicated very well with each other? Why?

_____

_____

What do you think are some common hindrances to communication between any two people?

_____

_____

Do you see any of these hindrances present in your own communication with each other? Explain.

_____

_____

KEY AREAS

Lets explore three key areas of healthy marriage:

Mentors focus on one or two based on the Growth Opportunities Analysis. The Let's Talk and Let's Kick it Up a Notch sections are designed for deeper digging into a skill or topic. Choose which sections to complete based on need and your own discretion.

1 OUR COMMUNICATION

2 OUR CONFLICT MANAGEMENT

3 OUR PARENTING

OUR COMMUNICATION: LET'S LEARN

We've shared some information about how bad communication is the leading cause of marital problems, but there is good news! We all have the capacity to grow in our ability to communicate and listen, so we need to want to improve our communication skills. The end goal of communication is for both partners to feel understood, and it takes two people to make that happen. Understanding requires both clear communication and active listening. Clear communication means sharing your honest feelings and needs with your partner. Active listening means not only hearing your partner's communication, but listening in a way that helps them know that they are being heard.

OUR COMMUNICATION: LET'S TRY

In a moment, we will have some opportunities to practice communication. We will ask a few questions for you to answer and discuss. There are some "rules" to consider as you share and listen, these "rules" are really just good habits for healthy communication and this is a good chance to exercise them.

Rules for Healthy Communication:

- Speak for yourself, use "I" statements and avoid "you" statements.

- No matter the question, try to be encouraging and graceful with your words.

- Be careful not to pass blame or responsibility all on one person or situation.

- Try to arrive at some mutual understanding, and maybe, come up with an agreed upon solution. You can always ask others for help in finding good, potential solutions.

- Do not allow yourself to be distracted. Determine a good place and time for the conversation that works well for both of you.

- Make eye contact and physical cues to show you are listening.

- Summarize what you heard both the thoughts and feelings involved, to clarify that you understand.

OUR COMMUNICATION: LET'S TALK

How would you describe your ability to clearly communicate and actively listen in your relationship?

_____

_____

What are one or two ways that you would like to see communication between the two of you change?

_____

_____

Are there any of the rules for healthy communication previously listed that would be especially beneficial for you, as a couple, if regularly applied?

_____

_____

OUR COMMUNICATION: LET'S KICK IT UP A NOTCH

This is a take home challenge. Find a time each day to answer the following questions. Take as much or as little time as you need, and be sure to remember the communication habits and rules for healthy communication from this session. Of those habits and rules, remember especially to encourage and be aware of how you communicate negative information.

What did you enjoy about each other today?

_____

_____

What was not as enjoyable about your relationship or day together?

_____

_____

What is one reason why you appreciate your partner. Explain why you picked that reason today.

_____

_____

SOMETIMES LOVE LANGUAGES CAUSE CONFLICT

My husband's main love language is Quality Time, which is a struggle for me because I am in a dead run most of the time. Sitting still with him on the couch requires conscious effort. My main love language is Acts of Service. My husband used to sit on the couch, frustrated because I was doing the dishes, packing lunches, and picking up toys while he was waiting for me to come sit with him. Finally, he realized that if he helped me with the chores it filled my love tank, and freed me up more quickly to be able to fill his. Sadly, this took years longer than it should for us to discover, so we are very upfront with other couples to learn to speak the other person's language as quickly as possible.

A STORY FROM A MENTOR COUPLE

OUR CONFLICT MANAGEMENT

Take the time to understand how your partner processes conflict. Learn to approach conflict in a manner in which your partner will respond the best and then be able to communicate clearly.

OUR CONFLICT MANAGEMENT: LET'S LEARN

It's important to understand that the presence of conflict in a relationship is expected. Experiencing conflict is not the sign of a doomed relationship. Many couples are afraid to address conflicts in their marriage until they find themselves hitting a boiling point, then all of their past frustrations erupt out at once and the situation becomes harder to resolve. So, when it comes to conflicts in a relationship, our focus should be on learning when and how to communicate in order to work through the conflicts together.

There are three helpful habits that will create a healthy environment for conflict resolution. The first is desiring resolution. It may sound simple, but desiring resolution can be difficult at times when our nature may want to punish or withdraw from each other. Desiring resolution means a desire to remain close and intimate with your partner, it is a dedication to your union. This habit is often found in the words of many couple's wedding vows, the promise to love each other through all seasons of life, even through major conflicts. Desiring resolution also can be a filter that helps us pick our battles; if we desire resolution then we may be less inclined to escalate minor problems into major conflicts.

The second helpful habit is learning how to recognize and address conflicts. There are times when the conflict is front and center or emerges from a direct conversation; it is easy to see because you are both right in the middle of it and it is happening right now. In these moments, it is important to recognize and communicate that there is a conflict that needs to be addressed instead of running away from the issue. Other times, conflicts can emerge when one partner is completely oblivious to it. One partner might be coming home with no idea that there is a conflict and find themselves getting cold shouldered or ostracized without understanding why. In these moments, it is important that the upset partner effectively and lovingly communicates the conflict and the unaware partner seeks to learn and understand the source of the conflict. If the conflict isn't shared then it can't be resolved. If you feel a distance between you and your partner, recognize that there is something wrong and address it.

Once you've recognized and addressed the conflict, you can now process the conflict. The goal is not to always agree. Sometimes, the goal is to learn how to constructively agree. The third helpful habit is discovering a process that helps you move forward towards peace and forgiveness. Define the source of the conflict, identify ways you each contributed to the problem, share possible solutions, and agree on how to work together to resolve the conflict. It may be necessary to wait and schedule a time to come back together to begin or resume the process; solving a conflict in a healthy and constructive manner is better than solving it as quickly as possible. The process is not meant for one person to win and one person to lose; it isn't a punishment. If you learn from an argument, you are less likely to have the same argument again. If you don't take the time to learn from the argument, history will repeat itself. The process of resolving conflict is a necessary tool for a helpful and healthy conversation.

OUR CONFLICT MANAGEMENT: LET'S TRY

In conflict there are Turtles and Hailstorms.

The turtle just wants do go into its shell when conflict arises. The more noisy the conflict the more the turtle wants to withdraw from the situation.

The hailstorm wants to deal with the conflict in a whirlwind of emotion right then and there as soon as the conflict happens. The hailstorm wants to pursue a conversation where he or she continuously rains down points and proofs about why their side is the best and most important.

In most conflict there is a pursuing hailstorm who attempts to rain down harder and harder while the turtle wants to withdraw deeper and deeper into its shell without dealing with the issue at hand. It is important to both deal with the conflict and to do it in a way both people can equally contribute to the solution.

In the midst of the hailstorm it is okay for the turtle to call a time out so they can process and come back to the conversation.

It is also okay for the hailstorm to call a time out and calm down before entering back into the conversation.

When a time out is called it is also important to schedule an appointment when the conversation can again be picked up.

Who are you in the conflict?

Who do you most relate to when dealing with conflict, the pursuing hailstorm or the withdrawing turtle?

_____

_____

What are some reasons why you want to resolve conflicts with each other?

_____

_____

What are some ways that conflicts impact you individually? (Do you shutdown, get angry, make excuses, feel distant, etc.?)

_____

_____

How do you recognize conflict?

Do you have a pretty good sense of when your partner is upset?

_____

_____

What are some physical or social cues that show that you're upset?

_____

_____

On a scale of 1-10, how quick are you to address conflict in your relationship? Explain.

_____

_____

How do you try to resolve conflict?

Are you typically ready to begin resolving conflict right away or do you prefer to schedule a time to come back together?

_____

_____

Are there places that you feel most comfortable processing conflict together?

_____

_____

What is most important to you when it comes to addressing and resolving conflict?

_____

_____

How do you forgive?

We all mess up from time to time. Sometimes we simply make a mistake and sometimes we make a conscious choice to behave poorly. The level of offense will often dictate the level of apology required when seeking forgiveness. Some of the most effective sentences to use when seeking forgiveness are "I'm sorry." "I was wrong." "Will you please forgive me?" Take a moment to each practice saying these phrases out loud.

Body language and tone are important if you want to communicate an attitude of humility and empathy. Avoid using the words "if" or "but" while apologizing (Ex. "I'm sorry if I upset you." Or "I'm sorry, but I was only reacting to what you just said."). Ultimately forgiveness is choice. When it is given there is always a sense of relief for both parties involved.

MENTOR US

Do you tend to use the words "if" or "but" when making an apology? If so, how do think you might break this habit?

_____

_____

How would you prefer your partner verbalize his/her regret differently? Explain.

_____

_____

Can you identify an area in your relationship where you have not given full forgiveness? If so, what is stopping you? Consider sharing future expectations and limits. Be specific.

_____

_____

THE S.H.I.M.L.Y. METHOD

We want to help shrink the amount of time it takes to recover from a disagreement and move past it. We use the S.H.I.M.L.Y. to help with that. S.H.I.M.L.Y. stands for See How Much I Love You. We have a token that says that, and we use it to remind the other person that we care. It often breaks the ice after an arrangement as well. When we want to make up but are not quite ready for words, we slip it into the other person's pocket or hand. If we are not arguing but want the other person to know we are thinking about them, we leave it in a shoe, on a keyboard, in the car, etc. to make the other person smile.

A STORY FROM A MENTOR COUPLE

OUR CONFLICT MANAGEMENT: LET'S TALK

Think of a recent conflict that the two of you shared.

Did you handle it well? Did you both desire resolution, recognize the conflict, and find a healthy process for finding a resolution?

How would you handle this conflict the second time around? Would you do anything differently if you faced this conflict again?

OUR CONFLICT MANAGEMENT: LET'S KICK IT UP A NOTCH

Challenge yourselves to practice these principles over the next two weeks. For example, try to determine what is happening in the moment when you feel yourself entering into a conflict. Verbalize it out loud. Examine yourself and how you are doing with recognizing the conflict, going through a process, and finding forgiveness. Then discuss with your partner how you feel you handled that most recent conflict.

OUR PARENTING: LET'S LEARN

How do you currently parent, or how will you parent in the future? When you communicate in parenting, it is always smart to be on the same page. Think about using the same terms and phrases so the children see you are in agreement. When you are not in agreement, buy yourself time; inform your children that you and your spouse will discuss the situation later. Referees always huddle up to talk before they make a call, you can too.

OUR PARENTING: LET'S TRY

Take a moment to work through these questions together. There is a section for couples who do not have children and a section for couples who have children.

Questions For Couples Without Children:

- Would you like to have children one day?

- If so, what kind of timeline would you like to have for your first child?

- How many children would you like to have?

- What are some goals you have as future parents?

- How will you support each other if timelines fail: children come early, late, or you find out that you cannot have children on your own?

Questions For Couples With Children:

- How would you describe the roles you each play in parenting?

- How in-sync are your parenting values?

- If you could adjust one thing about how your partner currently parents, what would it be.

Questions For Couples Forming A Blended Family:

In blended families, learning how to be a step-parent and dealing with ex-spouses can create added stress to your marriage without a plan. There are many situations that may come up that can cause difficulty for your relationship. (Ex. time-sharing arrangements/change of plans, ex-spouse disagreements, parenting style differences with step children, etc.)

Here are a few questions for you to answer:

- What will your role be (as step-parent) with regards to discipline with your step children and do you feel you have support from your partner?

- Are you, as a couple, making enough time for each other through all of the demands of parenting?

- Do you plan on having any more children?

- Do finances come up with regards to step-children responsibilities?

- Do you have any unmentioned concerns regarding your blended family?

OUR PARENTING: LET'S TALK

Were there any big surprises shared as you answered these questions?

_____

_____

Could you see your mind or heart changing any answers in the future?

_____

_____

Are there any parenting questions that you will need to revisit? If so, when is a good time to continue that conversation and move forward together?

_____

_____

OUR PARENTING: LET'S KICK IT UP A NOTCH

Pick two topics you want to further explore and discuss regarding parenting. Examples of topics might be discipline, how you as a couple will still make quality time for each other, dealing with ex-spouses or biological parents still in the picture, faith decision for kids, family schedules, etc. Write down your choices and sign your name to help remember your commitment to work together.

HOW DO WE MOVE FORWARD?

HOMEWORK

Think about and write down any questions or topics you want to be sure we talk about before your wedding?

_____

_____

CLOSING PRAYER

Before we depart let's close in prayer. Do you have any prayer requests?

_____

_____

A GOOD SUGGESTION

Between now and your next session, read through the following chapter and fill in as many answers as possible.

Our Love Life

CHAPTER FOUR

HOW'S IT GOING?

Welcome back to another session! We are entering the second half of this *Mentor Us* journey and have another important session to unpack together. Let's start out with a few opening questions.

Is there anything else you would like to share regarding your Communication that you did not get to share last session?

_____

_____

What have you been learning about yourself?

_____

_____

After doing your homework, are there any questions you want to make sure we answer or any topics you would like to discuss before your wedding day?

_____

_____

For our fourth session together the focus will be on our love life.

As we begin this session, it is important to recognize not everyone will immediately feel comfortable discussing affection, sex, and romance. We hope trust and respect have been built along our Mentor Us journey and we will be able to openly share with one another. What is shared in this mentorship setting will not be shared outside our mentorship. The truth is God created intimacy; He designed us to want it and to enjoy it. Let's talk about affection, romance, and sex.

ROMANCE

How would you define affection?

_____

_____

How would you describe romance?

_____

_____

Genesis 2:24, "That is why a man leaves his father and mother
and is united to his wife, and they become one flesh."

When it comes to our love life, sex gets all of the attention. We are fascinated and often obsessed with sex, and we should be. Sex is a gift from God. He created it, designed it, and has a perfect plan for it. The design for great sex and a fulfilling love life is more than just a physical act. There is more to it. The term "one flesh" which is used in the Bible gives us a picture of unity, an act that bonds two people spiritually, emotionally, and physically. The intimacy of marriage is greater than a physical act; it should also involve the connection of our hearts and minds through affection and romance. Sex is meant to be the celebration and expression of our emotional and mental connection. Physical and emotional intimacy must both be present for our love life to hold its true, designed value.

The radical difference in the way men and women approach romance and sexual intimacy sets the stage for possible clashes in marriage. They often have different definitions of great sex and fulfilling romance. If sex and romance are two sides of the intimacy coin, men and women tend to value each side differently. They may view one side as a reward and the other side as the cost.

Typically, the husband pursues romance based on his sexual passion, and the wife pursues sexual intimacy when she is really going after a romantic relationship. A woman's picture of romance and sex leans toward her emotional needs and her desire for a relationship with her husband. And yes, men have emotional needs; however, a man's desire for romance and sex is much more focused on a single experience: sexual affirmation. This isn't always the case for every man and woman; we are identifying where most people stand.

How do you typically romance a woman? Possibly surprise her with a date, a new outfit to wear, compliment her, remind her of how much you love her and what you love about her. Hold her hand, cuddle, bring her flowers. That sounds pretty good, right? But...when you want to romance a man? Bring food and show up naked.

It is important that you communicate your honest values and expectations to your partner so that you support and pleasure each other in your marriage. Both sex and romance are necessary to achieve intimacy in a healthy marriage, and knowing how your spouse functions and what works for them will help you make this incredible gift from God the best it can be for you both.

WHY IS ROMANCE IMPORTANT?

"The husband should fulfill his marital duty to his wife, and likewise the wife to her husband. The wife does not have authority over her own body but yields it to her husband. In the same way, the husband does not have authority over his own body but yields it to his wife. Do not deprive each other..." —1 Corinthians 7:3-5

God designed both the man and woman to be connected in every way; you belong to each other and are meant to help meet each other's needs. He wants to move us from pain to pleasure.

There are many reputable sources that claim more frequent sex is vital to a healthy marriage and actually provides various physical health benefits to you and your spouse. Ultimately, sex was designed to provide pleasure in our marriage and protection for our family. A healthy marriage provides a healthy foundation on which to build a healthy family. **God created marriage to provide a nurturing and loving family for children.** Physical intimacy between a married couple helps defend against temptations that threaten the fidelity of the marriage relationship, and it prevents the breakdown of the family unit. Again, physical intimacy is just one half of the equation.

Affection and romance are just as important to a healthy marriage. Just like sex, romance brings pleasure and protection into your love life. By understanding our spouse's romantic needs and making the efforts to meet them, we are bringing significant pleasure and health to our marriage. When we show affection to our spouse we are guarding their heart from anger, doubt, isolation, and temptation. The love and affection we display to our spouse helps prepare our hearts for showing love and affection to others. You may have noticed when a friend hasn't had enough sex or romance in their life, they are often in a bad mood and are likely to be difficult to work with or be around. Having more sex or going on a romantic date can be an easy fix to that situation.

Many of us learned habits of affection from our parents and family, this may have resulted in saying "I love you" at the end of every phone conversation or giving kisses when you get home from work. If your family wasn't very affectionate, then odds are that you are not very affectionate either. Because your marriage is yours, you and your spouse have the opportunity to determine how you want to show love and affection. That may mean redefining affection and practicing new habits or love languages. Doing this not only sets you up for a happy marriage but also allows you to better show love and affection to your family, friends, and even to God. As a result, your children will pick up your habits of communicating love and affection and will likely bring them into their future relationships.

"God blessed them and said to them, 'Be fruitful and increase in number; fill the earth and subdue it. Rule over the fish in the sea and the birds in the sky and over every living creature that moves on the ground." —Genesis 1:28

SATISFACTION The University of Chicago did a study and the information was published in an article called "The Revenge of The Church Ladies" – it stated that married Christians (especially Christian women) are having the most satisfying sex in the world.

UNHEALTHY SEX: THE TRUTH ABOUT PORNOGRAPHY

- 55% of married men surveyed view pornography every month. 25% of married women surveyed view pornography every month.

- 21% of Christian men and 2% of Christian women say they might be addicted to porn.

- Pornography use is correlated with a more than 300% increase in marital infidelity.

Pornography is statistically destroying intimacy within marriage. Instead of the husband and wife focusing on each other, porn moves the focus from "us" to "just me." The focus on your spouse is lost and the repeated use of porn takes precedence. Using porn to spice up marital sex is self-defeating. Instead of being more attracted to and engaged with one's spouse, the porn user will actually become more engrossed with the porn images. Studies show that when men and women were exposed to porn, they were less likely to be pleased with their partner's physical appearance, affection, and sexual performance.

The spouse of a porn user will experience feelings of hurt, betrayal, rejection, abandonment, loneliness, isolation, humiliation, jealousy and anger.

If porn is so destructive why do men and women keep watching it? Because it is so addictive! Unlike many activities, the use of porn releases a firestorm of chemical and hormonal rewards the brain records and remembers. The brain tells the porn user to keep coming back for the fun.

In addition, the explosion of the Internet makes porn viewing easily accessible, very affordable (most users view porn free online) and anonymous as users secretly view images on their Internet enabled devices.

Yet, God wants so much more for us.

"Marriage should be honored by all, and the marriage bed kept pure, for God will judge the adulterer and all the sexually immoral." —Hebrews 13:4

Great sex requires an intimate investment, and the rewards of intimacy have built-in multipliers. In addition to the connection of heart, mind and body, sex within the marriage provides emotional benefits (increases level of commitment, boosts self-esteem, lowers feelings of insecurity, and provides a positive outlook on life) and physical benefits (reduces physical illness, reduces risk of heart disease, lowers blood pressure, and improves sleep patterns).

If you or your partner struggle in this area there is help. Let your Mentor couple know and they will, without judgment or shaming, direct you to the right resources.

OUR LOVE LIFE

Our love life is important. We need to have some honest and open conversations about our expectations and desires for sex, affection, romance, and intimacy. The more we understand about our spouse the better we will be able to support and satisfy one another. Please take the time to work through these important questions together.

KEY AREAS

Let's explore three key areas of healthy marriage.

Mentors focus on one or two based on the Growth Opportunities Analysis. The Let's Talk and Let's Kick it Up a Notch sections are designed for deeper digging into a skill or topic. Choose which sections to complete based on need and your own discretion.

1 OUR INTIMACY

2 OUR FRIENDS AND EXTENDED FAMILY

3 OUR RELATIONSHIP WITH GOD

OUR INTIMACY: LET'S LEARN

Sexuality and affection are not the same, however, they are complementary to each other. When it comes to loving each other, both play an important role. We can identify sexuality as physical intimacy and affection as emotional intimacy.

Physical intimacy and emotional intimacy build off each other, they strengthen each other. Imagine the two batteries that go into your television remote: there is a "+" end and "-" end on each battery as well as marks on the remote that tell us how they should be positioned together. One end is not more important than the other, and the battery on the left is not more important than the battery on the right. The power and connection is found when both sides of both batteries find their place and work together. It is important to take time to understand the way your spouse gives and receives affection so that you keep a powerful connection. The more you understand how to love them, the better you are equipped with being able to meet their needs. We want to do our best to help meet our spouse's needs and being able to do this romantically will continue to keep you both connected.

OUR INTIMACY: LET'S TRY

Here is another chance to share and compare answers. Keep in mind, there isn't a best answer, this is meant to help each other communicate desires for sexuality and affection.

On a scale of 1-10 (very little to very much), how much verbal affection do you desire in your marriage?

HERS _____   HIS _____

On a scale of 1-10 (very little to very much), how much non-verbal affection, (such as hand holding, hugging, and cuddling) do you desire in your marriage?

HERS _____   HIS _____

On a scale of 1-10 (very little to very much), how much romantic dating, get-a-ways, or gift giving do you desire in your marriage?

HERS   _____   HIS   _____

On a scale of 1-10 (very little to very much), how much sexual intimacy do you desire in your marriage?

HERS   _____   HIS   _____

OUR INTIMACY: LET'S TALK

How was affection displayed in your family growing up? What kind of habits or love languages did your parents show each other and show you?

_____

_____

How did your family talk about sex: make jokes about it, pretend like it doesn't exist, warn against it, or talk openly about it?

_____

_____

As you move forward together, how can you show affection to each other based on your desires and love languages?

_____

_____

What kind of expectations do you have for sexual intimacy in your marriage?

_____

_____

OUR INTIMACY: LET'S KICK IT UP A NOTCH

This challenge is for a later time when the two of you can sit down in private and share with each other. These are important questions and it is important to make sure you are open and understand each other. It is also okay to set up times with your Marriage Mentors, male to male and female to female, to discuss and gain wisdom on these important topics.

- Have you fully shared your sexual history with your future spouse?

- Do you believe in contraception? Do you have any plans for birth control?

- What are your views on pornography?

- Do you have any fears regarding physical intimacy? If so, what are your fears and concerns?

- If you are having sex for the first time on your honeymoon, are there any questions or concerns you have?

- How do you plan on letting your spouse know your sexual desires and level of comfortability?

OPTIONAL GOAL SETTING FOR SEX IN YOUR MARRIAGE:

See if you can have fun agreeing on the number of times you would like to have sex in the first six months of your marriage, or an average amount of times per week or per month. What ever you decide should be a fun goal to strive for and not a mandated contract to hold over your spouses head. Couples who set goals tend to achieve more, even if they never fully accomplish the goals they have set.

OUR FRIENDS AND EXTENDED FAMILY: LET'S LEARN

A marriage brings together more than two people. You each bring relationships with family and friends, and with them can come their traditions, opinions, and schedules. A lot of people are brought together by association of your union; with them comes great strength and encouragement as well as the potential for frustration and trouble. Learning how to love your family and friends as a married couple is important, but it isn't always easy. The goal is to communicate well and establish healthy boundaries and balance. Friends and family should remain connected, don't lose sight of the support and strength they offer; and there should also be understanding, flexibility, and boundaries for your new home and life together.

It is always smart to have boundaries and limitations on your outside relationships. No other human relationship is more important and sacred than your marriage. Everything and everyone around your marriage will affect that relationship in a positive or negative manner. Boundaries are essential for growing in intimacy in your marriage.

OUR FRIENDS AND EXTENDED FAMILY: LET'S TRY

It is important to keep connected to your family and friends. Take a moment to work through these questions together:

On a scale of 1-10 (very little to very much), how strong is your connection to your family as you go into your marriage?

HERS _____ HIS _____

On a scale of 1-10 (very little to very much), how important are your family's opinions, traditions, and vacations going forward?

HERS _____ HIS _____

On a scale of 1-10 (very little to very much), how connected are you to your friends as you go into your marriage?

HERS _____   HIS _____

On a scale of 1-10 (very little to very much), how important are your friends opinions, influence, and social interactions such as girl weekends or guy trips to you?

HERS _____   HIS _____

OUR FRIENDS AND EXTENDED FAMILY: LET'S TALK

What are some ways that your families are similar or different from each other?

_____

_____

What are some of the opinions, traditions, or vacations that your family has that you definitely want to keep and repeat?

_____

_____

Are there opinions, traditions, or vacations that your family may pressure you to keep as you begin your new life together? How will you respond?

_____

_____

Are there any relationships with family members that may cause conflicts in your marriage?

_____

_____

Are there any friendships that may cause conflicts in your marriage?

_____

_____

How will you work through conflicts with family and friends?

_____

_____

Are you satisfied with your level of connection with family and friends? If not, which area could improve?

_____

_____

As a couple, how can you encourage each other to have healthy connections with family and friends?

_____

_____

OUR FRIENDS AND EXTENDED FAMILY: LET'S KICK IT UP A NOTCH

Managing closeness in your marriage will help with your management of other relationships. For this challenge, each of you will need to write down (separately) at least four actions/items that help you to feel closer or more connected to your partner. Then take turns sharing your items and writing them down on this page.

HERS

_____

_____

_____

HIS

_____

_____

_____

Were you surprised by how easy or difficult it was to do?

_____

_____

Were you surprised by any of your partner's answers?

_____

_____

The second part of this exercise is to 'put to work' those very important keys to maintaining your closeness. Make a list below of ways that you can make them happen in your everyday life.

HERS   HIS

_____   _____

_____   _____

_____   _____

The last part of your challenge is for each of you to choose two of your actions/ items and 'save the date' over the next month with your intentions to keep your connection going strong.

HERS   HIS

_____   _____

_____   _____

_____   _____

Make this a monthly habit and you will insure closeness in your marriage.

OUR RELATIONSHIP WITH GOD: LET'S LEARN

God loves you. The question is, "Do you love God?" Life events and family experiences can influence your answer. Your answer to this question will also influence your future family. The closer we grow in our relationship with God the stronger our love is for Him, the people in our lives, and ourselves. The more we are able to learn how God created us, we grow in our confidence which gives us the ability to love others more deeply. This all starts with a daily intimate relationship with God.

OUR RELATIONSHIP WITH GOD: LET'S TRY

How much do you know about your partner's relationship with God? Share what you think you know about each other's faith or lack thereof.

_____

_____

OUR RELATIONSHIP WITH GOD: LET'S TALK

What were you taught about God growing up?

_____

_____

Who is God to you?

_____

_____

What do you think happens when you die?

_____

_____

What do you think is the meaning of life?

_____

_____

What do you think is the purpose of marriage?

_____

_____

How do you think your relationship with God or lack thereof influences your relationship with each other?

_____

_____

OUR RELATIONSHIP WITH GOD: LET'S KICK IT UP A NOTCH

The key to paving the way to improving your spiritual path as a couple is having a plan and intentionality.

On a scale of 1 to 10 write down how you would rate your current status in pursuing God as a couple. A 1 being the lowest, meaning a growth opportunity and a 10 indicating you are doing very well.

	HERS	HIS
Prayer	_____	_____
Church Attendance	_____	_____
Giving	_____	_____
Bible Reading	_____	_____
Church Participation	_____	_____
Overall Rating	_____	_____

To solidify your work with action steps, choose one of your items and discuss more about how you would like to grow in your spiritual oneness.

Discuss and decide on one step to take that moves you closer to God and spiritual growth.

MENTOR US

HOW DO WE MOVE FORWARD?

First, let's celebrate your upcoming wedding.

Do you have everything you need from us (ex. marriage counseling certificate, contact info, etc.)?

_____

_____

In our first session together, we asked what you hoped to get out of these mentoring sessions. Do you feel that all your expectations were met? Is there anything else you would like to discuss or learn?

_____

_____

Think about when we can meet after your wedding. Mentors typically reach out to couples sometime after the wedding ceremony to see how things are going and to plan the next session together.

In our next session together, we will begin the process of building a successful marriage plan with a financial plan included. In the meantime, we want to map out a plan for your love life.

HOMEWORK

Having a healthy marriage is like having a healthy body. If you only go the gym once in a while and you don't eat right, your body will not be healthy. If you only work on your marriage on your anniversary and you don't work with one another to improve things, your marriage will get flabby. Continue to commit to specific times to work on your marriage.

Take turns mapping out six dates you would like to have in the next six months.

1. _____

2. _____

3. _____

4. _____

5. _____

6. _____

CLOSING PRAYER

Before we depart let's close in prayer. Do you have any prayer requests?

_____

_____

A GOOD SUGGESTION

Between now and your next session, read through the following chapter and fill in as many answers as possible.

The Wedding

CHAPTER FIVE

HOW'S IT GOING?

Here we are in session five! Congratulations to you, the new couple. We are so excited about this journey that you have just begun together. We are getting close to the end, and we have some important conversations ahead. But first let's discuss your wedding and how you have been since then!

What are your favorite memories from your wedding? Do you have any pictures or videos to share?

_____

_____

What is something that has surprised you since the wedding?

_____

_____

What have you been learning about yourself?

_____

_____

How is it really going... be honest.

_____

_____

Before we start on todays topic, do you have any questions?

_____

_____

For our fifth session together, let's focus on our plan.

Now that we can look back and celebrate your wedding, we want to encourage you to make a plan for moving forward. Whether it is regarding children, vacation, vocation or location we want to assist you in talking through a plan that is unique and tailored to your marriage and relationship. So today we will start the process of identifying growth areas, setting goals for a healthy marriage, and taking some steps in the right direction.

PURPOSE

Through good communication couples can discover deeper meaning and purpose as they move together in life. God has a purpose for your marriage and has given you the ability to communicate so that together you can follow that purpose and resolve conflicts along the way. Through the marriage relationship God moves us from meaninglessness to purpose. Your purpose as a married couple may look different from other couples you know. That is absolutely okay. The point is to figure out together your greater purpose through your marriage, and then live it out to fulfillment.

COMPONENTS OF OUR PLAN

When we first started this process back in session one, we began our mentorship by asking you to share your story. Our stories connect the past and present to the future and they connect and become a part of your story together. The mentorship journey is all about moving forward, and this is the time when you can map out where you want your marriage to go and how you plan to get there. There are five key areas that make up a good marriage plan, and they are the same five areas that make up your story. They are: family, foundations, friendships, faith, and finances. These five areas created a holistic story of your past, and will help you create a holistic and intentional outline for your future. As you address where you want to go, we can help you determine steps that will help you get there. Let's take a moment to examine these five key areas and understand what they represent in the future health and success for your marriage.

FAMILY   Family, by design, changes, and nothing changes your family more than marriage. Your family instantly grows through the addition of your spouse, and then brings the in-laws and extended family into the picture. You may want to have children together in the future, our have had children together already, or you may bring children from previous relationships. As time goes on, your family will continue to change in ways and at times you cannot predict. Having a plan for the future of your family helps you establish and promote healthy principles and goals along the journey of your new family's story. A future plan reinforces a healthy sex life, excellent parenting, and leadership and support within the home. It also pre-determines how you will both handle situations with your in-laws and extended family.

FOUNDATIONS   The foundations of your marriage will be a culmination of the values and traditions you bring from your past, as well as the values you establish now moving forward into your future together. This also includes how you decide to value each other. The foundations of your marriage will influence how you act and react to the people and situations around you. A strong foundation provides stability in hard times, patience and listening, support and understanding of each other's roles, and can help you maintain peace in stressful situations. A plan that strengths and secures the foundations in your home is vital for your future.

FRIENDSHIP   A long and healthy marriage requires a long and healthy friendship with your spouse. You don't stop dating when you get married. The truth is you still don't know everything about each other. Our wish for you is you never grow tired of growing closer together. A plan for friendship distinguishes how you will continue to pursue each other and learn more about each other's DESIGN. You will also establish and reinforce how you will handle close relationships outside of your marriage. Having friends is important and healthy. Yet you will need to determine boundaries and goals regarding friendships outside your home so they do not hinder your own marriage relationship.

FAITH   The first step for your future plan in this key area of faith is to determine the significance of faith within your marriage. Whether or not faith has been a pillar of your life in the past or present, it is important to communicate its value and presence within your goals moving forward. Attending church, joining a small group, and reading the Bible together are just a few ways in which you can love God as a couple. If faith is already present in your marriage, then a future faith plan for your marriage will allow your faith to grow even deeper as you take steps together in your relationship with God. A future faith plan for your marriage will also impact the faith and lives of your children. Being intentional about developing a faith plan ensures your marriage will reflect the significance of your growing faith.

FINANCES   Money influences many of the major decisions for your family. Being able to navigate through this topic of finances in a healthy way will be beneficial to the future success of your marriage. With a financial plan for your marriage you will discuss and determine what you want to spend, save, and give. It will allow you to develop a working budget for the future on the path to reaching your pre-determined financial goals. A financial plan establishes and reinforces the habits and disciplines needed to achieve those goals. It also helps identify wise people who can give sound financial advice when you need it. Many couples make financial mistakes early on in their marriage or enter marriage already having financial stress. It sets them back for a time. Developing a plan in this key area allows you to be proactive and do your best to stay ahead of your finances.

WHY IS OUR PLAN IMPORTANT?

Wouldn't it be wonderful if we could see into the future? If we knew what was going to happen then we could perfectly prepare for upcoming blessings, maybe even avoid potential struggles altogether. Unfortunately, we don't know what is going to happen in five or fifty years from now. However, planning allows us to capture an image of the future and bring it into our present plans and conversations. You won't know when an unexpected expense will surface, but you can financially plan to save for it. No one has absolute control over the timing of having children, but you can plan on how you will parent and love them. Neither you nor your spouse is perfect so one day, probably sooner than later, someone will upset the other person. You don't have to wait until then to decide how you want to communicate frustrations or concerns in your home.

The blessings of life are unexpected and undeserved, and that is why they are blessings. Rewards, however, are always sought after and earned. A loving spouse is a blessing; a healthy marriage is a reward. A healthy marriage requires a plan. The five key areas of our marriage will not improve or grow by accident. You might be surprised to discover how many lottery winners lose everything, but if you understand the importance of a plan then you shouldn't be that surprised. Good planning is more valuable than good fortune.

"Then God said, 'Let us make mankind in our image, in our likeness, so that they may rule over the fish in the sea and the birds in the sky, over the livestock and all the wild animals, and over all the creatures that move along the ground.'" —Genesis 1:26

God has a plan for your marriage. Within this plan lies purpose and meaning. As individuals you were each given a purpose to make a positive impact on the world. As a couple, God has a further purpose for your two lives together that will reap blessings for you and others as you live it out. **God created marriage with the intention that a couple would be able to contribute.** You were designed to make an impact on this world together in partnership. If you want to know the specifics of God's plan for your marriage, you will need to get to know God. Now is a great time to start asking God to reveal his purpose for your marriage as we evaluate the possibilities of your marriage plan and discover the best next steps for you to follow.

WHERE DO WE GO WITH THIS?

Remember your growth opportunities? Earlier in our *Mentor Us* journey, you completed an analysis to help discover opportunities for growth for you and for your marriage. As we begin to build a future plan for your marriage, are there new or existing opportunities for growth that you would like to further explore? Observe the following key areas and the questions they present. See if there are any questions or key areas that immediately stand out or interest you to explore at a deeper level.

Key areas to explore in the future:

FAMILY

- How will you have a healthy sex life?

- How will you parent?

- How will you handle difficult family dynamics with immediate or extended family?

FOUNDATION

- How will you better communicate successes, stresses, and problems in your marriage relationship?

- How will you clearly define and understand your roles within marriage?

- How will you handle conflict inside and around your home?

> *"Planning is bringing the future into the present so that you can do something about it now."*
>
> *Alan Lakein*

FRIENDSHIP

- How will you continue to date and grow closer to one another?

- How will you understand and respect your spouse's friendships?

- How will you balance time together and with other friends?

FAITH BACKGROUND

- How will faith play a role in your home?

- How will faith impact your family or children?

- How will you take steps to each grow in your faith?

FINANCIAL SITUATION

- How will you spend, save and give?

- How will you handle financial situations coming into your marriage?

- How will you reach your future financial goals?

> "Commit your work to the Lord, and your plans will be established." —Proverbs 16:3

"For I know the plans I have for you," declares the Lord, "plans for welfare and not for evil, to give you a future and a hope."   —Jeremiah 29:11

Each of the five key areas of your marriage can cause major stress in your home if there is not open communication and a working plan. In 2015, The American Psychological Association released a study that stated 75% of American families are stressed about their finances. As part one of our homework before our next session, spend some time mapping out a budget that falls in line with your future financial goals. Use the simplified budgeting exercise on the following page:

"Most people don't plan to fail; they fail to plan."

John L. Beckley

BUDGETING WORKSHEET

	WEEKLY	MONTHLY
Total Income	_____	_____
Total Giving	_____	_____
Total Saving	_____	_____
Total Spending	_____	_____
Loans/Debt	_____	_____
Health	_____	_____
Housing	_____	_____
Living Supplies	_____	_____
Transportation	_____	_____
Utilities	_____	_____
Food	_____	_____
Clothing	_____	_____
Fun	_____	_____
Other	_____	_____
Total Expenses	_____	_____

For more extensive budgeting we recommend using programs like Quicken, or online tools like www.mint.com, or joining Financial Peace University.

HOW DO WE MOVE FORWARD?

HOMEWORK

For part two of the homework, separately write down your top three key areas or questions from the *key areas to explore in the future* page that you think are worth exploring in the first year of your marriage. Once you have both written down your answers, try to come together as a couple and write down three top answers you both can agree upon. Meanwhile, the Mentor couple should complete the same exercise entering answers with the Mentee couple in mind. When we meet at our next session we will compare answers and see if we can collectively come up with the next prioritized steps for the Mentee couple in their first year of marriage. This will be the groundwork for *our plan*.

HER TOP THREE

_____

_____

_____

HIS TOP THREE

_____

_____

_____

OUR TOP THREE

_____

_____

_____

CLOSING PRAYER

Before we depart let's close in prayer. Do you have any prayer requests?

_____

_____

A GOOD SUGGESTION

Between now and your next session, read through the following chapter and fill in as many answers as possible.

Our Move

CHAPTER SIX

HOW'S IT GOING?

This is the final session of *Mentor Us*! Thank you for investing your time and energy into each other and into this process. We are near the end of this book, but nowhere near the end of this journey. Before we get into the last section, let's take a moment to catch up.

Is there anything else you would like to share that you did not get to share last session? Or any questions you did not get to ask?

_____

_____

What is the best date you have been on since the wedding?

_____

_____

How are you flirting and showing love to one another?

_____

_____

What have you been learning about yourself?

_____

_____

For our sixth session together, let's focus on our move.

After doing your homework, hopefully a next steps plan is beginning to come into focus. Once we know our next step, we then need to take it.

OUR MOVE

In the previous session, we discussed creating a plan for your marriage and future. There are five key areas that embody your life together; each holds specific dreams and desires for your family. Now that a destination is being identified, a path will begin to take shape that will help lead you there. This path contains your next steps for your marriage journey. Some paths may feel easier or more natural to you, others may be daunting or slow going at first. Either way, the goal for this session is to clearly identify your next steps as a couple and move you in that direction.

Discuss the results of your homework:

Share the results of part one of your homework with each other:

_____

_____

How easy was it for you both to agree upon the details of your budget? Why?

_____

_____

What did you decide for your financial goals?

_____

_____

What parts of your budget would you like to share?

_____

_____

Do you have any questions about the budgeting process?

_____

_____

Share the results of part two of your homework with each other:

What were the top key areas or key questions you felt were most valuable to learn as you move forward in your marriage? Why did you prioritize them the way you did?

_____

_____

Are there any growth opportunities not listed that you would both like to learn and improve upon? Explain.

_____

_____

While the initial steps in this mentorship are universal, the next step needs to be tailored to the couple. In other words, every couple has a unique story. Every couple needs to understand his and her design. Every couple has special communication styles, skills, and love languages. Every couple has their own favorite types of dates and intimacy. And every couple needs a plan moving forward. It will always be tempting to compare your marriage and next steps with the marriage and next steps of your friends or family members. However, it is important to understand and recognize that our marriages are all different and unique.

Together, you should identify the first step of your plan, and then you both have to actually take it. It's your move to make!

— WHY IS OUR MOVE IMPORTANT? —

Often the biggest obstacle in your way of growth and strengthening your marriage is you. You may talk all day about what you should do or could do. You may even get excited thinking about what your marriage might look like. However, if you never put any of those thoughts into actions, then there is no progress. Remember, growth doesn't happen by accident.

God created marriage to help teach us. It takes a great deal of maturity to make a plan, identify your next steps, and follow through on them. A healthy marriage requires a strong and growing commitment. Marriage requires commitment to each other and commitment to work on your growth areas. God wants to move us through marriage from an attitude of what is convenient to an unwavering covenant. A covenant is a lifelong commitment. Those marriage vows before God and witnesses sealed the deal on a promise that is not to be broken. The stability of that promise is the stability of your marriage and its future success.

God created marriage to last. Marriage is a marathon. It is foolish to expect that anyone can show up and run the race well to the finish without any planning or practice. You can establish principles and goals now that will withstand the trials and troubles of this life. God wants to move our mindset through marriage from the temporary to the eternal. God models this mindset in His enduring love and commitment to us. Here is a hint: Let God's love lead your life and you will have what you need to run the marathon well to the finish.

> *God wants to move us through marriage from an attitude of what is convenient to an unwavering covenant.*

Remember you will always have coaches and cheerleaders. Mentorship should always be a part of your life. As you grow and take your next steps, you will be amazed to find yourself in the position to come alongside a newlywed couple and encourage them in the future. Do not grow weary of doing what is right for your marriage and for your family. Enjoy the ride and take lots of pictures so that you can share your story with others.

What do you already know about God's love and its eternal value?

_____

_____

What do you think are some excuses, or obstacles that can get in the way of taking your next move as a couple?

_____

_____

WHERE DO WE GO WITH THIS?

Map it out. Figure out your next step.

Based on your previous prioritization, see if you can agree upon some of the additional steps after the completion of these sessions.

What do you all agree should be worked on first when it comes to building your marriage and future together?

_____

_____

Review potential growth options—small groups, church ministry, further mentorship and study, counseling, coaching, care groups etc.

You might want to do some research on book and curriculum options to aid you in your next step. (Order any materials needed to begin this next step. Or schedule any additional times to meet.)

- [x] FAMILY
- [x] FOUNDATION
- [x] FRIENDSHIP
- [x] FINANCIAL SITUATION
- [x] FAITH BACKGROUND

HOW DO WE MOVE FORWARD?

What have you enjoyed from this mentorship experience so far?

_____

_____

What has been valuable learning information as a result of this mentorship relationship?

_____

_____

Do you feel ready to move forward with a plan for your marriage? Explain.

_____

_____

Now, take a moment and celebrate! You did it! You took the time and invested effort to grow and go further on the journey as a couple. We hope you enjoy your next steps on this exciting journey.

CLOSING PRAYER

Before we depart let's close in prayer. Do you have any prayer requests?

_____

_____

Thank you, Mentor couple, for your willingness to share.

Thank you, Mentee couple, for your vulnerability to grow.

THE NEXT STEPS IN OUR MARRIAGE RELATIONSHIP

WHAT?

_____

_____

WHERE?

_____

_____

WHEN?

_____

_____

REFERENCES

Introduction
- "Marriage and Divorce" American Psychological Association, https://www.apa.org/topics/divorce.
- "Marriage and Mens Health," Harvard Health Publishing, last updated June 5, 2019, https://www.health.harvard.edu/mens-health/marriage-and-mens-health.
- Eric Schaal, "Consumer Reports Ranked These Cars Worst in Reliability for 2018," CheatSheet, June 8, 2018, https://www.cheatsheet.com/money-career/consumer-reports-ranked-these-cars-worst-in-reliability-for-2018.html.
- Doug Demuro, "Here Are 5 Recent Exotic Cars That Have Gone up in Value," Auto Trader, September 26, 2017, https://www.autotrader.com/car-news/here-are-5-recent-exotic-cars-have-gone-value-269365.
- Shawn Achor and Michelle Gielan, "The Data-Driven Case for Vacation," Harvard Business Review, July 13, 2016, https://hbr.org/2016/07/the-data-driven-case-for-vacation.
- Camille Preston, "Promoting Employee Happiness Benefits Everyone," Forbes, Dec 13, 2017, https://www.forbes.com/sites/forbescoachescouncil/2017/12/13/promoting-employee-happiness-benefits-everyone/#381f8f6e581a.

Chapter Three
- Survey Reveals #1 Reason Couples Divorce. (2013, November 20). Retrieved December 18, 2020, from https://www.huffpost.com/entry/divorce-causes-_n_4304466.
- Department of Family and Human Development, Utah State University, 2001
- "Handbook of Family Communication," by Anita L. Vangelisti. Family Communication," by Anita L. Vangelisti.

Chapter Four
- William R. Mattox, Jr., "Aha! Call It the Revenge of the Church Ladies," USA Today, (February 11, 1999).
- The Barna Group, "2014 Pornography Survey and Statistics," Proven Men Ministries, accessed June 7, 2018, http://www.provenmen.org/2014pornsurvey.
- Steven Stack, Ira Wasserman, and Roger Kern "Adult Social Bonds and Use of Internet Pornography," Social Science Quarterly 85, (2004), 75-88.
- Dolf Zillmann and Jennings Bryant, "Pornography's Impact on Sexual Satisfaction," Journal of Applied Social Psychology, (July 13, 2006).
- Sathiya Sam, "Porn is Affordable, Accessible, & Anonymous." xxxChurch, March 9, 2020, http://www.xxx.church.com/men/3-things-to-get-free-now.html.
- Sheri Stritof, "The Benefits of Having Sex More Often: Emotional, Physical, and Relationship Benefits of Frequent Sex," Very Well Mind, November 20, 2019, https://www.verywellmind.com/why-to-have-sex-more-often-2300937.

ACKNOWLEDGMENTS

Thank you to...

- Erica Goodlet, Dean Burmood, Emily Gardner, and Griffin Gilstrap for being the supportive and inspiring spouses we all needed in order to pull off the project.
- Jodi Costa for supervising the formatting of this book.
- Sarah Williams for formatting and editing this book into a masterpiece.
- Michelle Alexandre for being a great teammate and support on this project.
- Adrian Traurig for cover design.
- Karen Hoke, Nancy Wyse, and Jessica Conley for help with proofing.
- Jason and Dr. Christie McMullen and Tim and Diana Journy for contributing and refining many of the concepts within this book.
- Jeanmarc Alexandre from TalkEdits.com for help with book promotion.
- Scott & Kim Roper for proofing and strengthening many of the concepts within the book.
- Kurt Parker, Amos Pierre, Dean McSpadden, and Harborside Christian Church, as well as Tom Bates, Krystal Rapp, and Jessica Conley for inspiring, testing, and supporting this project.

— CHECK OUT HARBORSIDE CHURCH —

www.harborsidechurch.org

harborside
CHAPEL

www.harborsidechapel.org

www.harborsidemusic.com

AUTHOR: TOM GOODLET

Tom Goodlet is a best-selling author, pastor, and publisher. More importantly, he is a husband, a father, and a forever student of Jesus Christ.

Tom is married to his beautiful wife, Erica, and has three children, Parker, Mason, and Avri. He is the Associate Minister at Harborside Christian Church in Safety Harbor, FL. In 2019, Tom founded Two Penny Publishing (www.TwoPennyPublishing.com). This fast-growing publishing company helps authors get the book from their heart into their hand. Tom is also a certified instructor of Leader Effectiveness Training for Gordon Training International and Stickler Learning, where he equips organizations to build a positive work culture with increased productivity and profitability. Tom co-hosts the Potentialist Podcast with Dr. Raul Serrano, which helps listeners see and achieve their potential.

For more access to Tom Goodlet's books, workshops, and podcast, visit www.tomgoodlet.com

AUTHOR: CAROL BURMOOD

Carol Burmood is a Licensed Mental Health Counselor and has had the great privilege of coaching and counseling people for over 15 years. Her leadership in ministry for many years extended to women and couples teaching, speaking, and facilitating groups.

Carol has been married to her husband Dean for over 22 years. They journey in life with their daughter Ali, husband Stephen and three grandchildren, Ethan, Ella, and Emme.

Carol is passionate about impacting people's lives by helping them discover how to bring purpose-to-dreams-to-life. Working on the *Mentor Us* project engaged her experience and wisdom for couples on how to cultivate a healthy marriage map for their future. She has also written an interactional book to inspire people to live with intention and fulfillment!

To read more about Carol Burmood go to http://lifeimpactcoaching.us

AUTHOR: MATT GARDNER

Matt Gardner is a pastor, author, and ghostwriter. He is a husband to his amazing wife, Emily, and a father to three sons, Josh, Jack, and Camden. Matt and his family can be found at The Church at Severn Run in Severn, Maryland where Matt works as Lead Student Pastor. Matt loves serving the next generation, families, and young couples preparing for a lifelong adventure of faith and marriage.

Matt co-authored MentorU and has partnered as a ghostwriter to help create three best selling books. You can look forward to more writing from Matt through upcoming solo projects, contributions, and collaborations.

AUTHOR: HEATHER GILSTRAP

Heather Gilstrap lives in King, North Carolina with her husband Griffin and their five children. Her main focus is raising her children to be confident world changers. Heather serves alongside her husband, who is the senior pastor of their church. They also host a podcast together called The Real Marriage Podcast (www.therealmarriagepodcast.com). She is a freelance writer, blogger, and somehow in between it all she is writing books to inspire and encourage women to thrive in their life and grow in their relationship with Jesus.

Find out more at www.heatherlynngilstrap.com